MW01709086

CONVERSATION STARTERS

Arts Management Topics for Today

The Huffington Post Blogs

2009 – 2010

by Michael M. Kaiser

DeVos Institute
OF ARTS MANAGEMENT
at the Kennedy Center

THE DEVOS INSTITUTE OF ARTS MANAGEMENT
AT THE KENNEDY CENTER

The DeVos Institute of Arts Management at the Kennedy Center
2700 F St., NW
Washington, DC 20566

Manufactured in the United States of America
Typeset in Mrs. Eaves

Library of Congress Control Number: 2011923048

Conversation Starters: Arts Management Topics for Today, The Huffington Post Blogs 2009–2010
by Kaiser, Michael M.—1st ed.

Summary: *Conversation Starters: Arts Management Topics for Today* is a compilation of blogs written on topics of arts management.

ISBN # 978-0-9833379-0-4

TABLE OF CONTENTS

Introduction

Since mid-2009 I have had the distinct pleasure of serving as a weekly columnist for the Huffington Post.

Each of my posts is fewer than 600 words in length. The topics I introduce typically deserve more in-depth treatment than I can give in this limited amount of space.

As a result, I like to think of each column as a conversation starter rather than as the final word on any given topic.

While I never intentionally try to stir controversy, I have found that many of my entries have started intense, passionate discussions amongst my colleagues.

My posts on the future of modern dance, cultural diplomacy and the challenges facing American orchestras have caused particularly high levels of comment and discourse.

My post on my apology to my colleagues has received more 'hits' than any other. I know my approach to arts management, which puts a premium on revenue enhancement rather than cost reduction, frustrates many in the field.

I hope this volume of selected posts from 2009 and 2010 encourages additional discussion.

Arts management is a young field. There is much we all have to learn. And learning must be fostered by informed, intelligent debate.

THE CYCLE

Over the course of the past 12 months I have developed a model that describes how arts organizations can successfully fill the income gap so well described by Baumol and Bowen in their seminal text, *Performing Arts: The Economic Dilemma*.

This approach, which I call 'the cycle,' is predicated on the development of important, exciting and engaging programming. If that programming is well marketed (both programmatic marketing that helps sell tickets and institutional marketing that builds visibility for the organization as a whole), the organization's family of ticket buyers, donors, board members and volunteers will grow and will become energized.

An energized family creates revenue for the organization — both earned and unearned — that can be invested in future exciting programming. If this new programming is marketed aggressively, the family grows larger and more engaged, producing more revenue that can be invested in even better programming, etc.

This healthy, self-reinforcing cycle reveals the linkages between the key operating areas of an arts organization: programming, marketing and fundraising. It also suggests the dangers of an approach many organizations take to balancing budgets: Cutting programming and/or marketing too drastically results in the family losing interest and looking elsewhere. This leads to lower revenue and more programming cuts.

Several of my columns discuss issues with elements of this cycle, though none with the cycle itself. Stay tuned!

Arts in Crisis

American arts organizations are threatened; but it is not the economy that poses the largest threat.

It is the decision-making of boards and staffs in response to economic challenges that has much greater long-term implications for the health of our arts ecology.

While arts funding only fell 6 percent last year, many arts organizations are making drastic cuts to their programming. Many have cancelled performances, eliminated educational programming, shortened seasons or closed altogether. Others are "dumbing down" their product; there is a widespread call to make programming more accessible (read boring). Still more are cutting their marketing dramatically. After all, they argue, who will notice if we spend less on communicating our (reduced) programming?

These approaches to dealing with the current recession all assume that cost is the underlying problem of the arts; conventional wisdom suggests that an arts organization can 'save its way to health.'

But this is wrong, dangerously wrong.

Arts organizations across the world have a revenue problem, not a cost problem. We are a remarkably efficient industry, doing more with less. But we do not yet know how to create the revenue streams we need to do our work in a consistent manner.

And what creates revenue for an arts organization? Good art supported by strong marketing. Arts organizations that consistently do good work and are aggressive about their marketing are the ones that succeed, both programmatically and financially.

Cutting programming and marketing, the current favored strategy, therefore, ensures that future revenue will fall. This initiates a vicious cycle — less art and marketing yielding less revenue leading to more cuts in programming and marketing, less revenue, etc. etc.

Taken to its conclusion, an arts organization simply gets too small to matter.

This is why our arts are in crisis today. We can survive the current economic downturn if we keep our programming vital and work harder than ever to convey our message. Those arts organizations that compete well will survive and recover when the economy recovers. Those that continue to cut away at their programming are likely to become irrelevant.

Are We Forgetting the Mission of the Arts?

Over the past 25 years, I have bristled when anyone says or writes that arts administrators have taken over the arts and that artistic initiatives are taking a back seat to financial concerns. I feel slighted. My work, and the work of my fellow arts managers, after all, is aimed at finding the resources necessary to allow the artists to do their work. If we are not successful, there will be neither the donors nor the audiences required to fund the artists.

But I must admit that the more I travel around the nation and the world, the more I realize that money concerns truly have begun to overwhelm artistic decisions in too many arts organizations. The fear that the organization will not survive has driven many arts organizations to produce safer, more accessible and, unfortunately, more boring art, especially in this current economic downturn.

This is a deeply scary phenomenon. If arts organizations do not take risk, they cannot create the next great work of art. If not-for-profit arts organizations begin to think like for-profit entertainment companies, we will not produce the next generation of great playwrights, composers, artists and choreographers.

It is already difficult to tell the difference between many not-for-profit theater companies and their for-profit counterparts. Not-for-profit organizations receive a tax advantage because of our educational role, our ability to take risk and our missions that place artistic accomplishment above financial reward. Yet too many of us are ignoring these objectives.

This is not just an American problem. The larger amounts of government funding available in other countries should, and do, allow arts organizations to make bolder choices than their U.S. cousins. But the level of government funding is shrinking in most countries, and arts organizations are struggling to find ways to build audiences and attract private donors. Once again, playing it safe is becoming a favored approach.

I understand the motivation. The arts suffer inflation more than other industries, and no one is providing us with a cushion to protect us if a risky project fails in spectacular fashion. It is scary to be responsible for the salaries of so many people with so little money coming in. But I also understand that without risk there cannot be art and that the organizations that do the most innovative and exciting work will also have the biggest financial rewards and thus, ultimately, the most stability.

At the Kennedy Center, I know that I need to achieve fiscal balance every year. But it is not accomplished by selecting only safe works. I think of every season as if it were a stock portfolio, balancing the riskier projects with safer, more accessible programs. This season, for example we have a large *VSA* festival devoted to artists with disabilities and are co-producing a world premiere play by Terrence McNally. Neither project is assured to be successful. These are balanced by productions of *Mary Poppins* and *A Streetcar Named Desire,* starring Cate Blanchett — two sure winners. If every season does not have a few wonderful, surprising moments, then I will not be able to maintain the interest of my large donor and audience bases. Without their support, we obviously cannot continue to build a larger, more diverse calendar of performance and educational programming.

When I hear artists evaluating a project based on audience size, a project's attractiveness to donors and other measures of financial success, it makes me sad. While every artist must be realistic about the fiscal implications of a given work, this should not be his or her primary concern. We need our artists to be thinking expansively, to be challenging themselves to be truly creative and to be challenging their administrators to find the resources required.

But boards and administrative staffs have bullied their artists and dulled their creative impulses.

Maybe money is taking over the arts after all.

The Big Project

In these difficult economic times, many arts organizations are working hard to develop programs that do not require many resources. Board members are pressing for small operas, small plays and small ballets. Many executive directors, understandably concerned about balancing the books at a time when contributed income is still in jeopardy, are concurring.

Unfortunately, these smaller projects, while good for the annual budget, rarely do anything for the image of the organization or its long-term financial health. They rarely excite audience members, donors, board members or the press.

Why does this matter? Because the programming of an organization, and the excitement it generates, is central to the fundraising capacity of the organization. Fundraising is not about board members forcing their friends to contribute; this brute-force form of fundraising is rarely sustainable.

The most consistent, faithful donors are those who are excited and surprised by the work of an arts organization. And when the organization is regularly producing large scale projects that attract a great deal of public and press attention, more and more of these donors are likely to become affiliated. Artistic ventures that change the way a community views an organization, therefore, are a strategic, mission-driven way to build financial health.

When I arrived at the Kennedy Center in 2001, during the last period of economic instability, we announced the largest project in our history: a landmark celebration of the works of Stephen Sondheim.

We did this project because we had a point of view about the work. We believed there were many myths about this work that were simply not true. There should always be a curatorial reason for doing any project. Simply 'filling a slot' is not good enough.

But we also did this project because I knew that we needed to excite our constituents. We had not produced our own theater at the Kennedy Center for over a decade. We needed to do something to make the press and the public sit up and take notice.

The Sondheim Celebration generated an astonishing amount of press and public interest in the Kennedy Center. It was the opening salvo in a series of projects that were large in scope and true game-changers. Projects focusing on the works of Tennessee Williams, the arts of China and the plays of August Wilson were other mega-projects we mounted over the past nine years.

These projects are expensive. They cannot be developed in a few months; one must plan years in advance to engage the right artists and to attract the necessary resources. But when they do come together, the impact is spectacular and long-lasting. Eight years after the Sondheim celebration, it is still written about and remembered by our growing donor base.

At this time of tightened budgets, arts organizations must continue to develop these mega-projects, perhaps for implementation three or four years from now when there is more funding available. Just talking about projects in advance can generate excitement and have a positive impact. Those who think big at this time, when so many others are thinking small, will recover more quickly when the economy turns around.

Why the Arts Don't Pay for Themselves

One of the questions I receive most often whenever I write about the arts is, "Why can't the arts pay for themselves? Why are public or private contributions required?" (These questions are frequently asked in far more colorful language.)

There is a simple answer rooted in two economic problems that affect all arts organizations.

The first, and most problematic, is that arts organizations have a very difficult time achieving productivity improvements. Most every other industry improves worker productivity annually. This is crucial because productivity improvements mitigate the impact of inflation.

But arts organizations have a difficult time improving the productivity of their performers, typically the largest expense item for an arts organization. Orchestras do not play Beethoven's Ninth Symphony faster every year. We do not have fewer performers in *Hamlet* than when it was written hundreds of years ago. A Balanchine ballet that required 32 dancers in the 1950s still requires 32 dancers today.

As a result, costs go up more quickly in the arts than in other industries because we do not accommodate some of the impact of inflation with productivity improvements.

This problem with escalating costs is compounded by the second economic problem faced by arts groups: Once a theater or gallery is selected, one has literally set in concrete the real earned income potential for the organization; one simply cannot sell more tickets than one has seats.

This means that expenses continue to rise while real earned income is held steady. This creates an income gap that continues to grow over time.

How can we fill that gap? The primary approach has been to raise ticket prices. The problem is that we have raised prices so high that we have disenfranchised too many potential arts patrons. When people say the arts are irrelevant, I have to disagree: The arts are simply too expensive. Whenever we have free performances at the Kennedy Center the performances are filled — especially for symphony and ballet.

Price increases have become a bigger problem given the emergence of so many inexpensive electronic substitutes. For the price of two of the best seats to the Metropolitan Opera, one can now buy a computer and watch Maria Callas and Joan Sutherland on YouTube for free.

Another approach to filling the income gap has been to start auxiliary businesses, though few if any arts organizations have been successful balancing the books with unrelated business income.

The only other choice open to not-for-profit arts groups is to raise money from government and private donors. In this country, unlike the rest of the world, the vast preponderance of money contributed to arts groups comes from private sources — individuals, corporations and foundations. Our Puritanical heritage still influences the degree of federal government support for the arts; the notion that music and dance were evil meant that the federal government did not directly support artistic endeavors in a substantial way.

The rising importance of contributed funds is a result of the increasing size of the income gap. It is a problem that will not go away and requires more and more sophisticated management of arts groups.

That is why I started the Kennedy Center Arts Management Institute and why I have lobbied for two decades for more funding for arts management education in this nation. We spend so much training young singers, dancers, musicians and actors and spend so very little training the people who will employ them — and who face a growing income gap that simply won't go away.

Revisiting Baumol and Bowen

I had the pleasure of visiting beautiful Princeton University on my 50- state tour. My "Arts in Crisis" session took place at the beautiful McCarter Theatre, one of the great university-affiliated theaters in the nation.

While preparing for my presentation, I could not help but reflect on the remarkable contributions two former Princeton professors, William Baumol and William Bowen, have made to the field of arts management.

It was Baumol and Bowen, writing in their seminal text, *Performing Arts: The Economic Dilemma*, who identified the central economic challenge of the arts: our inability to improve worker productivity. Published in 1966, this book could arguably be called the foundation for the field of modern arts management.

The two professors identified that costs rise so quickly in the arts because we cannot perform *Hamlet* with fewer players than when Shakespeare wrote it, nor do we play Beethoven's Ninth Symphony faster and faster every year. As a result of this productivity challenge, our costs rise more quickly than in other industries. Coupled with the lack of real earned-income growth once we fill our theater, the performing arts face economic challenges unlike most other industries.

How to fill this gap between rising expenses and fixed earned income has been the challenge to every arts manager for centuries. Our solutions have not always been satisfactory or ultimately helpful to our organizations or our field.

The traditional approach to filling this gap was asking for government subsidy. The amounts given by government agencies in the United States were relatively modest; those given in Europe and other parts of the world often account for two-thirds of the budget of major arts organizations. This has proven to be an inconsistent fix, at best, in recent times, however. Not only are most state agencies cutting their arts support during this economically challenging time, but most international governments are doing so as well.

The approach to addressing our 'income gap' most in vogue for the past 30 years has been to raise ticket prices. Unfortunately, in doing so, we have priced so many people out of our performances that we are considered irrelevant by many. We are not irrelevant. We are simply too expensive. And with electronic substitutes increasing in number and decreasing in cost, we are also in danger of permanently losing attendance at live events, as people become more and more addicted to their personal screens.

Many boards have encouraged not-for-profit arts organizations to explore the creation of new earned-income businesses to cover rapidly increasing expenses. Unfortunately, virtually all of these endeavors are either too small or too risky to be long-term contributors in major ways.

The only fix that seems to have long-term potency is to continue to build on the level of contributed income. While this is an unpalatable solution to many, I have no doubt that 30 years from now, the level of contributed income as a percent of total income will grow substantially, not just in the United States but also across the globe.

Don't blame me. Blame Baumol and Bowen!

The Power of Celebrity

It is astonishing how much power celebrities have to create interest and excitement for an arts project.

When a world famous actor or dancer or singer is involved in a production, the ability to raise money and sell tickets rises immeasurably.

And when a major exhibition by a celebrity artist is opened, the lines to enter can be very long indeed. Parking and food service revenues naturally rise as well, and the sale of tickets and gift shop items increases substantially.

The challenge for so many of us in the fields of classical music and opera today is that the number of celebrity artists is dwindling. This is not a comment on the quality of today's performers. There are amazingly talented young performers in every art form. But the vast reduction in recording activity has cost the classical music field its best marketing partner. Record companies used to spend substantial sums to make their artists famous. Almost none of this activity happens anymore. In addition, the reduction in mainstream press attention to the arts has made it difficult if not impossible to become a star. As countless newspapers fire their arts journalists, it is difficult for an artist to build a reputation for excellence.

Think of the opera singers I heard in one season at the Met 30 years ago: Leontyne Price, Joan Sutherland, Birgit Nilsson, Montserrat Caballé, Marilyn Horne, Luciano Pavarotti, Plácido Domingo and Sherrill Milnes! They all had major recording contracts and were written about in leading publications across the globe. These were artists with international renown who could sell out the largest opera houses, even in non-standard repertory.

The number of opera singers who can do that today can be counted on two hands. And the number of these singers who are under 40 years old doesn't require a second hand. It is getting tougher and tougher to count on the power of a celebrity opera singer. The same is true for classical music conductors and soloists. No wonder opera companies and symphony orchestras are having challenges selling high-priced tickets.

To make matters worse, the negative impact on fundraising is just as substantial as the impact on ticket sales. Many donors want to support organizations that can boast of famous performers. And those organizations that can make these stars available to donors at receptions, dinners, lectures, etc. have a true advantage in building a fundraising effort, especially among individual donors. When there are fewer celebrity artists, fundraising revenue is bound to suffer.

This forces individual opera houses and symphonies to create fame for their guest artists in their home markets. This is not impossible. But when an artist is only present for a few performances, it can be difficult to justify a large expenditure of money for creating fame.

Major arts organizations are going to have to spend more time creating excitement for the organization as a whole so they can depend less on the reputations of their individual artists. This will be a substantial challenge. Arts managers will face new and difficult challenges in the future.

What I Learned from *Ragtime*

Having the Kennedy Center production of *Ragtime* mounted on a Broadway stage has been both exciting and an honor. This was the first Kennedy Center musical that was transferred to Broadway. The chance to show our work to a larger audience was truly rewarding for all of us involved.

It was also an educational experience for me.

I have learned to appreciate how much easier it is to sell a show when it is produced by a not-for-profit institution than when it is a stand-alone, for-profit venture, as most Broadway shows are.

When a not-for-profit institution opens a show, we have already pre-sold a substantial sum of tickets to our subscribers. Most of our subscribers have tickets for the first few weeks of a run; this gives us more time to build public awareness, through advertising and word of mouth, for the later weeks when more single tickets must be sold. We also have ongoing marketing channels including newsletters, magazines, websites, and e-communications. The Kennedy Center News, a bi-monthly magazine, regularly reaches 250,000 households alone; our website receives more than five million visits a year. These modes of communications are invaluable in explaining a production, offering group and other discounts, and showcasing the reviews of critics.

When a Broadway musical opens, the marketers must start from ground zero. There are no subscribers; every ticket sale is a single or group ticket sale. There is no loyalty to the producing entity. Excitement about the show, and revenue, must be established from scratch. The first few weeks are not filled with subscribers; one has to find ways to pack the initial houses. And an open-ended run means that one has to sell so many more tickets than the limited runs typically mounted by not-for-profit theater companies.

The not-for-profit institution also has name recognition and a loyal audience base; many ticket buyers are happy to trust the Kennedy Center or Goodman Theatre or Signature Theatre.

Only a few knowledgeable theatergoers really know the names and reputations of the producers of Broadway shows. And these days there are so many names above the title that it is hard to decipher who truly is in charge.

Perhaps the major exception to this rule is Disney, which operates like an institution. Many ticket-buyers are happy to trust a Disney production, just as they are happy to trust a not-for-profit institution. And while Disney does not have subscriptions, it certainly has the communication channels that are far more potent than even those owned by the largest not-for-profit theater companies.

It would not surprise me to see theater owners and producers collaborating in the future to create mock 'institutions' that can establish permanent brand names, mailing lists, websites and newsletters that emulate their not-for-profit cousins.

It would make their lives easier and their productions cheaper.

As for me, now that *Ragtime* has closed, I am going to go kiss my marketing department!

Why Ticket Prices Must Change

The central challenge facing arts managers is to fill the ever-widening gap between rapidly increasing expenses and earned income, primarily from ticket sales. This gap continues to grow each year since the number of seats we have to sell does not increase but expenses do.

Unfortunately, the favored technique used to fill budget gaps has been increasing ticket prices. When we increase prices, typically at budget time, we hope that a small increase will not be noticeable and we need the added revenue to break even. However, we have been doing this for so long that tickets prices are now too high for many people to afford regularly. It is not unusual to see tickets for major opera companies cost $250 or more, and the best theater tickets are now well over the $100 mark in many cities. For two tickets to an opera, you can now buy a computer and watch Leontyne Price and Joan Sutherland on YouTube for free!

No wonder so many people have stopped going to performances. A recent study by the NEA showed that a huge number of people are getting their arts exposure online and fewer are coming to the theater. No wonder so many arts organizations are suffering. Without audiences we receive no ticket revenue, and the audience members we lose cease to donate as well. The claim that the arts are irrelevant is getting difficult to dispute.

The arts are not irrelevant. I observe this every day during the Kennedy Center's free Millennium Stage performances that attract hundreds of audience members each night with minimal marketing. Our annual Open House in September features performances on each of our stages all day, for free. The most popular events? Ballet and the symphony, which conventional wisdom says are the most irrelevant of all.

If we want to keep, not to mention rebuild, our audiences, we need to rethink our ticket prices and to find other ways to balance our budgets.

We need to find productive ways to lower our costs. Cutting programming is not a good solution, but establishing creative joint ventures and reducing infrastructure are.

And we need to work actively and aggressively to increase fundraising revenue (by producing exciting work and marketing that work well) and use a portion of this revenue to lower ticket prices.

We do not need to lower the prices of all tickets, however. We find that the buyers of the higher price tickets are less price sensitive; they will buy at any cost. That is why the premium price tickets on Broadway continue to sell.

But the audience members who buy lower price seats tend to be very price sensitive; reducing the price of these tickets should have a big impact on audience size.

If we don't, we will find ourselves with fewer and fewer people in our audiences and an ever-smaller donor base. The arts will, at best, become the exclusive province of the elite, and to the vast majority of people, live arts will become irrelevant.

Free Performances vs. Complimentary Tickets

I have often railed against the practice of giving complimentary performance tickets to lots of people who feel they deserve them. Too many arts organizations, especially those in foreign countries, make a habit of handing out large numbers of free tickets to donors, friends, government officials and virtually anyone who asks for them. Ironically, these 'comps' are typically offered to those who can afford to buy a ticket rather than to bring those unable to pay into the theater.

This practice always leads to the same problem: People come to expect free tickets and refuse to pay for performances now or in the future. As a result, the earned income enjoyed by these organizations is substantially less than it should be. (Many of the beneficiaries of these free tickets come to think of the performances as valueless and refuse to become donors as a result!)

There are times when free tickets are justified: when they are part of the package of benefits promised to a donor who makes a substantial contribution, when they represent professional courtesy (allowing fellow artists or arts managers to see your show) or when papering the house to make it a better experience for those who have paid for their tickets. Although when papering, it is important to offer free tickets to those not in the main audience prospect pool. One doesn't want potential ticket buyers waiting for free tickets to future performances.

However, while I am opposed to free tickets, I am a big fan of free performances. That might sound like a contradiction but it isn't. When an arts organization has a mission to provide access to the arts for everyone, it will frequently plan for one or more free performances in a season. These are mission-driven events. They indicate that the organization wants to make sure that all parts of the community can participate.

In many communities, arts organizations offer free performances in public parks, especially in summertime. This gives people a chance to experience an arts event and to test their interest in a given art form. It is particularly meaningful to people who might not otherwise be able to afford entry into ticketed events.

The Kennedy Center has been offering a free daily performance for nearly 14 years on our Millennium Stage. Literally millions of people have had the opportunity to see a performance that they might not have otherwise enjoyed. This access is an explicit part of our mission; as the national cultural center we believe we are obligated to serve all constituencies, including those who cannot afford a ticket. But we would not offer free tickets to everyone to our paid performances. In fact, we hope that many people will be exposed to a given art form through our free performances and choose to come to ticketed performances in the future.

Every organization I have counseled to reduce the number of complimentary tickets has suffered some adverse audience reaction for a short period of time but has reported a dramatic increase in earned income. Changing the rules has been of great benefit for these organizations. And some of the extra money earned has been available to support free performances for those who really need them.

The Kennedy Center's 2010 Season

Last Tuesday, the Kennedy Center announced its 2010–2011 season. It includes a broad mix of accessible and challenging art, theater, music and dance, American and international performers. Everything from the debut of the National Symphony Orchestra's Music Director Christoph Eschenbach to a new production of Sondheim's *Follies*, from a Festival of India to a celebration of the 50th anniversary of the inauguration of President Kennedy. The range of artists appearing is startling: Renée Fleming, Mariinsky Ballet, Bill T. Jones/Arnie Zane Dance Company, Patti LuPone, Anat Cohen, Lang Lang, and Peter Brook, among many others.

I had the idea to announce our entire season at once when I first arrived at the Kennedy Center in 2001. In prior years, every art form announced its programming separately. As a result, the press, public and donor attention was minimal. I believed that the richness of our programming was only evident when you examine the entire array of artists and art forms.

Today, our press announcement is a major event on our annual calendar. The list of over 1,000 performances we produce and present — there are another 1,000 performances presented by others — is eagerly awaited. We have a donor event the night before in my apartment to give a few major sponsors a preview of the season. My entire staff joins the press in our Family Theater to hear the announcement, which is broadcast live on the Internet. And a lunch is held immediately after where the press can discuss the season with our numerous programmers.

Why is this relevant to anyone but the Kennedy Center? Because it is an inexpensive event that builds our reputation and our sense of community. The staff is energized, the press is (hopefully) impressed, our donors feel special and proud, and the richness of our programming is on show for anyone who cares to visit our website. (We also e-mail a season advertisement to hundreds of thousands of members of the community.)

Any arts organization can create an event that does not cost much but adds to institutional image. It need not be a season announcement. It can be a lecture or master class series, an exhibition from the archives, a performance at an important local political event or a local sports hero participating in an educational event or.... The limit is only the creativity, connections and assets of the organization. The visibility of the project can have a major impact on the way the organization is perceived and therefore on its revenue potential.

But beware. No one event has a sustaining impact. We must create the next project and the next and the next. I believe that every small or mid-sized organization should have three or four truly special events a year; larger organizations need one a month or so to build enough interest. If we can do this consistently, the 'family' we build grows, as does our vitality.

I am confident that our season announcement last week will help us create the revenue we need to implement it. Now we move on to the next event, and the next, and the next.

The Concept of Family

Many boards of directors, seeking a measure of fiscal stability, hire corporate executives to run arts organizations. A large number of these executives quickly fail as arts leaders. They either decide that the arts are not for them or are asked to leave after creating tension within the organization.

One of the reasons for this high rate of failure is clearly the difference in mission between corporations and not-for-profit organizations.

The very words "for profit" define succinctly the true mission of every corporate entity. Despite the flowery words in their annual reports, all corporations aim to create the highest stream of profits possible to maximize share price. This is their obligation and their true mission. They may say publicly that they "bring good things to life," but they really hope to bring good things to their shareholders.

Arts organizations and other not-for-profit organizations, however, only know what they are "not for." What they are for — their missions — can vary widely from one organization to another. The way they measure success is clearly different from a corporation and from each other. Therefore, the way they plan and operate must also be different.

When corporate executives become leaders of arts organizations, they must truly appreciate this difference in mission or they will come into severe conflict with their artists, staff and board members.

But I believe there is a more subtle reason why many corporate executives fail as arts leaders.

Arts organizations are large families. Our artists, staff members and board members form the heart of our families. But there are many other members of our families: donors, subscribers, volunteers, etc.

Most of our family members are not paid. In fact many provide resources to the organization. They do this because they believe in our missions, enjoy their participation and are excited about our plans for the future.

Our family members become especially productive when they are happy. When they lose interest, they look elsewhere to participate. Successful arts leaders know how to engage members of the family in planning activities and key projects. They know that it is important to share information rather broadly to keep family members feeling involved and important. They invest time, often good amounts of time, to make sure that the family is as happy, and productive, as possible.

Corporate leaders are not used to this way of working. They are used to compensating everyone involved in the organization. The most productive employees are promoted and earn bonuses and salary increases.

Corporate leaders, therefore, need not provide the same level of psychic reward as arts managers, and they don't need to be as collaborative or collegial.

Many highly successful corporate executives get leadership positions in the arts (and other not-for-profit entities) and ignore their family members. They make changes they believe are vital without thinking about the way family members will react.

When these decisions cause problems in the family, there can be many ripple effects: Donors can reduce their giving, volunteers can depart for other organizations, staff can resign and board dissension can develop.

Not every corporate leader falls into this trap. But any arts board that hires a corporate executive to run its institution should be on the lookout for this problem in waiting.

The First Big Grant

One of the exciting moments in the life of a young, small or mid-sized arts organization is when it receives its first, large foundation grant. This grant, a recognition of the good work already being performed, typically allows the organization to expand its programming. New staff may be hired, new space may be rented and sometimes even a building is purchased. But in virtually every case, the infrastructure of the organization is expanded.

The sense of validation that accompanies the awarding of the grant can be moving and life-affirming. After years of struggle, a major funding body has recognized your work. The promise of things to come is almost as exciting as the initial grant.

But as exciting as this moment is, and as helpful as it is to have guaranteed funding for a number of years, there is also a hidden pitfall that too many arts managers ignore: The grant will end.

Too many organizations that receive this first big grant build the infrastructure to support their new, increased programming without thinking about the day the grant period ends. It seems so far off, after all.

But the day does come when the grant is over, and most foundations do not renew their grants automatically. Most organizations don't have a plan to deal with the reduced level of income and don't think about it until that day arrives. By then it is too late. The organization has built an infrastructure but no longer has the foundation grant to support it. All too often, programming has to be slashed, staff has to be laid off and not infrequently, the health of the organization is placed in jeopardy.

This can be a traumatic moment for any arts organization.

I have long lobbied foundations to make their grants to smaller organizations in the form of challenge grants. A challenge grant must be matched by other contributions, often by new gifts or increased gifts from existing donors.

By forcing the organization to build a new, larger donor base *during the grant period,* the transition when the grant is over is eased. The foundation's money might be gone, but the new donors attracted by the match help fill the void.

But many foundations simply do not want to do the oversight work required of administering a challenge grant. And if the foundation is not far-sighted enough to give a matching grant, the organization must be disciplined and smart enough to create its own challenge grant. The senior staff and board must use the grant period to build its donor base. A serious, concerted effort to attract new donors must be pursued. The foundation grant gives the organization an imprimatur that can attract new donors.

It is so easy to relax after winning the first big grant and to allow the nascent development effort to lie fallow. But you do so at your peril. It is never fun to get smaller, especially after the successful conclusion of a grant.

Responsible Philanthropy

A great deal has been written in recent weeks about the new English government's plan to slash government funding for the arts. Understandably, the arts organizations in England are deeply concerned. They have relied on government funding for large portions of their budgets and do not feel equipped to fill the budget gap that will result from this sudden reduction in income. This is not a unique situation. Governments and other major institutional funders across the globe are cutting arts funding as other social needs take precedence.

This situation inevitably leads to a discussion of the responsibility large donors bear when they wish to cut their grants substantially. Do they have an obligation to prepare their grantees for the bad news? Do they bear responsibility for the health of their grantees after the grants are reduced?

If a funder truly cares about the arts (or any sector of the not-for-profit sector it funds, for that matter), it should do three things:

1. Reduce the size of grants over a period of time. A one-time cut does not give the affected organizations the time they need to find alternative sources of funding. If a donor can announce its reduction plan in advance and spread the cuts over a number of years, the grantees have time to reduce budgets, at worst, or find alternative sources, at best.

2. Give challenge grants that force the organizations to develop new sources of revenue. A challenge grant is a grant that must be matched by other donors. If receiving a grant is dependent on raising matching funds from new donors or increased grants from existing donors, the organization will be in a better position to survive the cuts. This is especially important for smaller organizations that might not have the experience or capacity to raise money from private donors. A challenge grant is true, positive motivation to build this expertise.

3. Give arts organizations training in marketing and fundraising so they are better prepared to find new revenue. In many countries where fundraising is still a new concept, most arts organizations have no experience raising private contributions. Simply telling these organizations to find new sources of support is equivalent to telling me to perform an appendectomy. I would not know how to begin. Training is available to help organizations begin the process of building private contributions.

Donors, especially governments, have an obligation to behave responsibly. Sometimes donors are forced to reduce their grants, but this must be accomplished while giving grantees the best chance of surviving and thriving despite these cuts.

But arts organizations, themselves, are responsible for their long-term fiscal health. No arts organization should be so heavily dependent on one donor that a cut from that donor threatens the organization's existence. Arts organizations in every country, no matter how much the government gives, should diversify their funding sources as insurance against sudden cuts from any source. Just ask the leaders of any arts organization in England if they wish they had spent more time over the last decade building a larger cadre of private funders.

Does Size Matter in the Arts?

One of the frustrating responses I receive to my "Arts in Crisis" presentations is that my recipe for success only works for large organizations in big cities.

I could not disagree more. I believe that planning far in advance is more important for smaller organizations than larger ones. Smaller organizations have a harder time developing the large, transformational projects than larger organizations. That is why they tend to remain small. If they take the time to plan large, exciting programs four or five years in advance, they would be far more likely to find the resources they require to mount these programs. This would allow them to build visibility in the community, attract stronger board members and increase their ability to generate resources. Planning should not be left to the larger groups.

And institutional marketing is also more important for smaller groups since they tend to be less well-known, their programmatic marketing campaigns are smaller and their projects tend to be of smaller scale.

The challenge is to determine which assets the organization possesses that can help build reputation. Is it a major production planned for the future? Access to important artists or politicians who might participate in events? A rich history that deserves a museum or library exhibition? An invitation to perform at an important festival? An opportunity to participate in a highly visible special event? A major announcement of a new program or grant? A special anniversary that can be celebrated?

The list of possibilities is endless.

It is up to the creative manager to use these assets to create a visibility *campaign* for the organization. No single special event or announcement will build institutional image enough to make a difference. All good marketing requires repeated 'hits' with a given message. A small or mid-size organization should be making news at least once a quarter; larger organizations need many more exposures a year.

The small organization may not get on a national television show, but the number of people it must influence is fewer than for a big organization. In fact, most arts organizations must really only influence 100–200 selected people in their communities to have a life-changing effect on the organization. Making a list of these individuals and working aggressively to influence them is more important than appearing on late night television!

There are many smaller, regional organizations that have created great art and visibility and give testimony to the power of programming planning and institutional marketing in smaller markets.

Perhaps my favorite example is Glimmerglass Opera in Cooperstown, New York, which produces very well-regarded opera performances in an opera house built in a town of fewer than 3,000 residents. People travel from far and wide to attend performances at Glimmerglass. The organization does not shy away from difficult operas or unusual interpretations.

If Glimmerglass Opera can build an international reputation for excellence, your organization can too, no matter where it is or the size of its budget. Begin to plan your art farther in advance and take time to find the resources needed for projects that will energize your audience and donor base. And initiate an institutional marketing effort that encourages new people to enter your organizational family.

Size doesn't matter in the arts.

The Power of Joint Ventures

In my travels across the nation I have been hearing a lot of discussion about the glut of arts organizations and the need to "thin out" the field.

This scares me greatly. I am certain that those proposing reducing the number of arts organizations have in mind eliminating those that are weakest. Who, after all, would want to eliminate an arts organization that is producing good art and sustaining itself financially?

No, reducing the ranks really means getting rid of those arts organizations that are fiscally weak and that are viewed as a burden to donors and board members. But the weakest arts organizations are not always those that are producing the worst art; nor are financially strong arts organizations always the ones producing ground-breaking art. What if the Alvin Ailey organization had been "thinned out" in 1991, another recessionary time? Instead it turned around to become one of the strongest arts organizations in this nation.

Instead of eliminating arts organizations, I think we need to find ways to make existing organizations stronger and better able to support themselves.

My prescription, that good art, abetted by strong marketing, helps to create health, is viewed as a contradiction by some. How can a sick organization develop important art when it does not have sufficient resources to make payroll?

One approach that works well is to form a joint venture with another organization. A joint project can create important art while reducing the cost to each participating organization.

When I arrived at ABT in 1995, we were truly destitute, but I announced the largest artistic venture in our history: the first commissioned full-length ballet to a new score. We were able to find a partner, San Francisco Ballet, to share the costs of producing Lar Lubovitch's *Othello*. We each got to present this new work but only paid half the production costs.

Not every joint project must be pursued with a similar type of organization. Hubbard Street Dance Chicago and the Chicago Symphony Orchestra entered into a joint venture in 2004. Each year, Hubbard Street performs with the orchestra on one of its programs. This gives the CSO a chance to diversify its programming while Hubbard Street has a chance to associate itself with one of the world's great orchestras. This arrangement has led to a number of other engagements for Hubbard Street with the St. Louis Symphony, the National Arts Centre Orchestra in Ottawa and at the Hollywood Bowl.

Joint ventures can also be formed with non-arts organizations. The Ailey Company entered into a joint venture with Fordham University in 1992. Ailey dancers got to take college credits at Fordham and Fordham students could fulfill physical education credits at the Ailey School. Both organizations benefitted from the relationship.

Building a good joint venture takes time and effort. I believe it takes at least one year prior to the start of a project to develop the concept, create the venture, write the contract and ensure that both parties are benefitting.

Taking time to develop a clear contract that establishes the responsibilities of both parties is especially important. Who controls the art? Who controls the budget? How are potential cost overruns communicated and resolved? The world is littered with joint ventures that ended bitterly because one side spent more than budgeted and did not communicate the overruns in a timely manner to the other partner.

But a well-formed joint venture is one important method for building both artistic health and fiscal viability, especially in troubled times.

Cost Containment Matters Too

I have spent so much time in my career talking about the importance of increasing revenue by creating exciting art and marketing that some people believe it is all I think is necessary to run a successful arts organization. This is clearly not the case. There is a wide range of requirements for managing a healthy arts institution, from developing a productive board to inspiring staff and maintaining the facility to reaching out to the community. The list is a long one, and arts managers must be able to focus on many issues at once.

Because I stress the importance of building revenue, many people believe I am not interested in the other side of the profitability equation: cost reduction. I have often written that one cannot save one's way to health in the arts, and I mean it. I have yet to see a struggling arts organization turn itself around simply by reducing cost. Health in the arts is tied to increasing the amount of both earned and unearned income.

But I also know you cannot remain a healthy arts organization if cost control is ignored. For me, it is a way of life.

The cardinal sin in the arts is to waste. Wasting money, wasting time or wasting opportunities cannot be tolerated in a resource-constrained world. If one can accomplish a task for less money and doesn't, one is reducing the amount of resources that can be devoted to other important projects that help the organization achieve it mission.

Cost control can be achieved with budget cuts, of course, but far more effective in the long term is developing a culture that supports and rewards saving money against budgeted expenses. All staff members must understand that they make a direct contribution to the health of the institution when they save money. (Of course, if everyone on staff consistently spends less than is budgeted, there is unnecessary padding in the budget. While this might seem beneficial, padding budgets is dangerous because it artificially reduces the amount of mission-focused activity an organization pursues.)

But when staff members make an effort to spend less than is budgeted, through good planning or negotiations with vendors, the amount of money released for other activities can add up quickly. Particularly in bad economic times, arts organizations can bargain with vendors to achieve cost savings.

My staff is very familiar with my ardent desire for cost reduction. I joke that I squeeze every nickel until the buffalo poops. And I do. I have yet to find a budget that I cannot cut. I find waste and inefficiency everywhere.

But I also know organizations that focus only on cost containment can become depressing places to work. Artists, staff and even board members must appreciate what the organization is doing to increase the revenue, build an audience and expand a donor base. Cost containment must be part of the equation, but it cannot be the entire equation.

Ben Franklin was right. A penny saved is a penny earned. It just isn't as much fun.

PLANNING

Anyone who knows me knows that I am, at heart, a planner. Planning eliminates waste, and arts organizations have nothing to waste. Every dollar, every minute is precious. A good plan also ensures that everyone in the organization is headed in the same direction, that every participant knows what he or she is expected to accomplish to ensure the implementation of the plan, and it builds confidence among potential donors and board members.

Yet while so many arts organizations devote time and energy and resources to their planning activities, there are major deficiencies in most arts plans. First and foremost, too many plans for arts organizations ignore specific choices for future artistic projects; others are so general they amount to little more than a wish list.

When staff and board members believe the plan they worked so hard to develop has little real value, planning backlash, the feeling that less planning is better than more planning, develops. It is not surprising, therefore, that I write frequently about planning.

The Planner vs. The Entrepreneur

Everyone who knows me well knows that I am, at heart, a planner. I plan everything I do, often very far in advance.

I have spent much of the last two years trying to convince arts organizations to plan their art four or five years in advance. I believe that this time frame gives the organization the time it needs to find resources, create excellent art and attract an audience.

Virtually every project we mount at the Kennedy Center was planned five years before it is on one of our stages.

While I can argue for the virtues of this approach, there are many who question whether I am giving up on spontaneity, the great opportunity that emerges or works that didn't even exist five years ago. In other words, am I sacrificing my ability to be an arts entrepreneur if I plan so far in advance?

It is a good question with a simple answer: I do not believe there is a natural tension between being a planner and an entrepreneur.

The best planners know that their plans must be adaptable to change. If something changes in the environment, the strategy must change as well. It is only those who use planning as a crutch to provide order to their lives who hang on for dear life to a plan that no longer makes sense.

I always say I write my plans in pencil. While I have every intention of seeing my plans come to fruition when I develop them, I also know there is a likelihood that not every plan will be implemented, that some better opportunity will arise or some external factor may not allow for the quality of implementation I would have wanted and expected.

In fact, from my experience, the great entrepreneurs were all planners. They had a very clear idea where they were heading. But they were happy to grab opportunities that arose to make the end-point achievable.

While it may be each of these opportunities is how the casual public judges the entrepreneur, the more careful analysts see a trend to the projects that were selected and to those that were rejected.

What planning does is provide the highest odds that a project will happen — and happen well; what entrepreneurialism does is to ensure that the best projects are selected for that moment in time.

The combination is potent. Some big, complicated projects get planned far in advance. They are pursued with a consistent fervor that is required to make them happen. And more immediate opportunities are seized upon to complement these major projects. This past season the Kennedy Center mounted major festivals of gospel music and of arts by artists with disabilities. Each of these projects took many years of planning, which paid off handsomely. But we also presented the play *Thurgood*, which was offered to us just a few weeks before we announced our season. It was a smash hit. And we mounted three special performances to celebrate the arts in America this July that were planned only weeks before. Our season would have been the poorer without any of these projects. The balance between planning and entrepreneurialism certainly benefitted our audience.

What Is Missing in Too Many Strategic Plans

Recently, I was asked to meet with the board and staff leadership of an arts organization that has made great strides over the past two years.

In this turbulent environment, this arts center has strengthened its board, created new earned income programs and cut costs in ways that are transparent to its donors and ticket buyers. The accumulated deficit has been reduced, and there is a new spirit of optimism among the board members, staff members and artists of the organization.

But our meeting was still disturbing to me. When the group presented its plans for the next three years, there were proposals for creating a sizeable cash reserve, revitalizing the gift shop and catering operations, completing a substantial debt reduction program and building more aggressive programmatic and institutional marketing campaigns. Each of these plans was clearly outlined and admirably thought through.

But there was one substantial hole in their plans: There was absolutely no mention of artistic or educational initiatives.

How was this organization going to raise the money required to build its cash reserve fund or reduce its deficit without creating the programming needed to entice new ticket buyers and donors? When I raised this concern, I was told there were ideas for new programming but they were not formed well enough to be mentioned in the plan.

The following week I taught a group of arts managers in one of our regional capacity-building programs. The topic was planning. I asked allparticipants to share the section headings of their plans. They had sections on Missions, Goals, Objectives, Marketing Plans, Fundraising Initiatives and Financial Forecasts. But not one of the groups had any specific artistic or educational programming plans.

I asked all of the groups to read their mission statements. Every one of them was focused on artistic and educational programming. But as these groups did their planning, there was no explicit link made between their missions and their strategies.

How can one have a mission related to dance or theater or music but have no specific plan for programming?

How can one have marketing, fundraising or financial plans that are not based on the future work of the organization?

There is clearly a misunderstanding in many organizations about the role of the mission. Missions drive the entire planning process. The only reason to write a plan is to create a road map for achieving the mission. A plan that does not include specific programming is a meaningless document.

When we fail to recognize the primary role of programming in our strategic plans, we are implying a lack of trust in the value of the work we do in the arts. Good artistic and educational programming is not simply an expense that must be compensated with ticket sales and fundraising; good programming is the primary driver of revenue and, therefore, of fiscal health.

No wonder so many artists accuse arts managers and boards of ignoring the art in favor of financial concerns. It is right there in our strategic plans.

Why All the Booing?

I was fortunate to be invited to the opening of the Metropolitan Opera two weeks ago. The new production of *Tosca* made news when the production team was greeted by a chorus of boos when they bowed at the end of the performance.

I was surprised not so much by the boos as by the press coverage. Over the past 30 years of opera-going, I have seen many new, adventurous productions greeted by jeers when they debut. (Who can forget the reaction to Sir Peter Hall's *Macbeth* at the Met in 1982?)

For some reason, when directors approach favorite operas with a fresh perspective, audiences get angry. Perhaps it is the high ticket prices. Perhaps it is the fear that this new approach will become the norm and all opera productions will be similarly challenging. Perhaps it is the fear that this is the last production of the opera one will ever see.

I am fortunate to be able to see many opera productions, so perhaps I do not represent the average audience member. But I, for one, enjoy when a director takes a new approach to a work, as long as it is faithful to the music and makes sense.

When I ran the Royal Opera House, we created a new production of *Tristan und Isolde* that was very unusual. Tristan and Isolde each 'lived' on a boat that glided across a clear black (plexiglass) sea. They lived in their own worlds and never touched. I thought the director, Herbert Wernicke, had a beautiful concept. The production was not as well sung as I would have liked; I felt this undercut the director's concept. I expected negative reaction to the singing; the press, however, took after the production. One journalist called it "the lowest point in the history of the Royal Opera House." Wow.

I enjoy a beautiful, highly realistic production (*pace* Franco Zeffirelli). But I also enjoy a high-concept production when it is executed well; it forces me to examine the opera is a new way.

There was much to like in Luc Bondy's production of *Tosca*. Though ultimately I did not find it entirely persuasive, I particularly enjoyed the way the production put the relationships among the three principles in the spotlight. I believe Peter Gelb is doing what must be done by engaging important directors to create new productions; no performing arts organization can survive simply as a museum for beloved productions. And it takes courage to present a new production that is clearly going to be controversial on opening night.

But even if one did not enjoy this production, and even if one felt angry, booing seems to be an overreaction. Making art is about taking risk. Embarrassing serious artists when they are taking important risks seems hardly a smart approach that will foster additional experimentation. Next time you don't like a production, go home and write a blog.

Artistic Planning Can't Be Rushed

I recently participated in a very important discussion with my 10 DeVos Institute Fellows. The subject was artistic planning. The fellows had already heard me speak about the virtue of planning artistic ventures multiple years in advance: how it makes it easier to attract the artists with whom one wants to collaborate, how it assists fundraising and marketing, how it helps to secure touring engagements and how it helps to ensure that the mission of the organization is truly reflected in its programming.

But this discussion was about something more important.

It was about how planning art years in advance allows artists and arts managers to think and delve and angst and study in an effort to create truly important and surprising art.

I find far too many arts organizations take the artistic planning process too lightly. They take only a few hours to pick repertory for the following season. They think about what has worked elsewhere and copy it. They sometimes even wait until the subscription brochure is about to go to the printer before making selections.

The leaders of these organizations forget that the selection of repertory is a crucial element in achieving mission, building inroads into the community and achieving fiscal stability. They are so involved in implementing the programming they (hastily) announced the previous year that they spend no time planning for future seasons. As a result, their offerings do not change very much from year to year. They have similar resources to spend every year (if they are lucky), and the performances or exhibitions are not dramatically different. Not surprisingly, over time, their donors and audiences grow bored.

Of course there are those rare geniuses who appear to announce a wonderful season every year with little thought. But these geniuses are really planning all the time. Their minds are constantly sifting through ideas, selecting those that are most enticing and discarding others. They simply are not sharing their thoughts with others until it is required.

Most of us can't do this. We need time to consider myriad ideas, big and small, ambitious and simple. We do this every day, always on the lookout for the next great idea. One never knows where or when a great idea will emerge, but we have to be open to it. We need to share ideas with others, get their feedback, rethink projects that seem too risky or not interesting enough on reflection. We also need to think through the many aspects of implementing each project so we can determine which are most likely to be successful. And we need to think about ways to make the project more exciting and important; which auxiliary elements can be added — lectures, demonstrations, special events, etc. — that will make the project especially substantial.

If we fail to do this, we are abdicating our vital role as leaders of taste. We will not bring the new and exciting and different to our audiences.

If we simply program to meet a sales budget or to program what everyone else has found successful, we are not really being *arts* managers.

The Messiness Ghetto

I recently taught a seminar for board members in South Africa. I find that we offer far too little training to people who are meant to govern our arts organizations. While I have often taught similar sessions in the United States, this was my first such program overseas.

It was a spirited discussion, as these typically are. As in many countries, the role of the board in South Africa is evolving as the way arts organizations are funded is evolving. Board members, who traditionally were simply there to oversee financial health, are being asked to play a more central role in resource-gathering as private fundraising becomes increasingly important to the survival and growth of arts organizations.

My seminar was aimed at helping board members make this transition and at explaining to arts managers what they must do to motivate their board members to ask for funds. When board members are excited by programming and marketing plans, feel close to the organization and are allowed to view the creative process, they become far more successful as solicitors.

But I could not immediately identify one underlying anxiety that filled the room. I only realized after the session, on the drive to the airport, that the tension in many arts organizations, and between many boards and staffs, is often caused by the messy nature of art creation.

One does not make art neatly. Ideas emerge, they are challenged, changed and dropped. Many artistic creations, and certainly almost all performing arts ventures, are collaborative processes where each participant is experimenting, changing, dropping and trying again. This takes time, iteration and experimentation.

This activity does not lend itself to the strictures of planning. And artists naturally rebel if a board attempts to make them create work in a straight line.

; managers know how to segment off this part of the work from the 'ganizational efforts. They know how to plan for this messiness owing the organization to plan and market and create resources.

The fact that it is messy to create a new ballet does not mean that planning for the creation of that ballet has to be an unstructured process and cannot be accomplished smoothly. Nor does it mean that marketing and fundraising cannot happen in an orderly way in service to this messy process that actually provides the lifeblood of the organization.

When administrators and boards try to avoid the messiness, they ignore the mission of the organization. When board members argue that it would make more sense to become "more efficient" in the art-making process rather than expand fundraising goals, they are demonstrating a lack of understanding of the way art is created and the purpose of the institution as a whole.

But learning to accept how art is made and to embrace it and then to pursue everything else the organization does in a more structured, programmed way is central to success – in Cape Town or Washington, D.C.

Why We Use the Full Orchestra

There is a disturbing trend in the American musical theater. Producers are reducing the size of orchestras for most revivals, and new musicals are being written with smaller ensembles versus the large-scale orchestras that I grew up expecting to hear in the theater.

I appreciate the pressure to reduce costs of production. Anyone working in the live performing arts appreciates that because we do not increase productivity year in and year out, as other industries do, the arts suffer from a higher rate of inflation than in other sectors. There are no fewer roles in *My Fair Lady* than when it was written. And we do not perform *Fiddler on the Roof* faster every year. As a result, costs rise very fast in the live performing arts.

This problem is exacerbated by another economic reality. Because we do not add seats to our theater every year, our real earned income does not grow. Once we fill the seats in the theater, there is no way to increase real ticket revenue. These two problems create a growing gap between expenses and income. It is no wonder so many Broadway shows are forced to close prematurely. Unless every seat is filled, with modest expenditures on marketing, the costs overwhelm the income.

In an effort to fill this gap between expenses and revenue, producers have pursued two strategies: raising ticket prices and lowering costs.

Unfortunately, ticket prices on Broadway have been raised so often that most people cannot attend the theater regularly. This has reduced the pool of potential ticket purchasers substantially, raising the costs of marketing.

So naturally, attention has turned to ways to reduce other costs.

But cutting the size of the orchestra and replacing acoustic instruments with synthesizers does not only reduce cost; it also reduces quality. Some of the audiences may be fooled, but an ensemble of nine instruments cannot produce the same sound, the same overtones and the same sense of excitement as an orchestra of 28.

The glory of some of the recent revivals on Broadway — *South Pacific* and *West Side Story* come to mind — is that a full orchestra is employed. The feeling one gets simply from hearing the orchestra tune before the curtain rises is an integral part of the magic of live theater.

Unfortunately, to sell higher price tickets, producers have had to resort to stunt casting, bringing major stars from movies and television; in many cases, to pay these celebrities and the high costs of sets, costumes, stagehands, etc., producers are sacrificing the music in musical theater.

Too many not-for-profit theaters have followed this trend. It is now considered acceptable to perform the great works from the musical theater canon with tiny ensembles and electronic sound. We are in danger of undermining the quality of one of America's great contributions to the world of the arts. At the Kennedy Center, we use the original orchestrations for every musical we produce. Just as we would not reduce the size of our National Symphony Orchestra or cut the number of swans in *Swan Lake,* we will not reduce the orchestra size for *Mame* or *Ragtime* or *Sweeney Todd*. Our audiences have come to expect the true sound of a musical. It is time for others to follow suit.

An Implementation Plan

One of my favorite management tools is the implementation plan I develop to support my strategic plan.

An implementation plan breaks each strategy into identifiable steps, assigns each step to one or more person and suggests when each step will be completed. For example, if one strategy is to create a membership campaign, one step might be to design a membership brochure. This project might be assigned to a member of the marketing or development staff and might be planned for completion in December of this year.

If there is no effective method to carry out the strategic plan, the strategic plan is likely to collect dust and can lead to planning backlash, the feeling that planning is a waste of time. In an industry where the scarcity of resources is always a key limiting factor, good planning is essential.

However, creating an implementation plan is challenging. It requires the planner to identify each step required to mount a particular strategy. This activity in itself is a good test of the plan. If one does not know how to implement a given strategy, then the strategy is likely not going to be implemented.

Creating an implementation plan does far more than simply test the ability of the organization to make a strategy happen, however.

If one simply sorts the implementation plan by person, one has a list of the steps assigned to each staff or board member. These are their individual strategic work plans. Each person now knows exactly the role he or she plays to implement the strategic plan. If one person's list is too long, perhaps that person has been assigned more than can reasonably be handled and the strategy is in jeopardy. If someone has too little assigned, then that person may be able to handle more of a load. In any event, this sort allows the manager to communicate with each person so that everyone knows what they are meant to accomplish and then to make sure every job has been completed on time.

But one can also sort the information in the implementation plan by completion date. This gives the staff and board leadership a strategic timetable. At any point in time, leadership can determine whether every step has been completed that was meant to have been completed. If tasks have not been completed on a timely basis, management must determine why. Did the strategy change? Did other events prevent timely completion? Did the project simply fall through the cracks? Does this imply other changes in the planning calendar must be made?

Too often arts boards simply approve a plan and then ignore it. Too many board meetings never refer back to the plan that may have taken substantial time to develop. The implementation plan gives the board a tool to keep track of the progress toward implementing the plan. Each board meeting should include a review of the implementation plan. What has been learned to date? Should the strategy be adjusted in some way?

I could not manage my organizations without my implementation plan.

Why I Hate Board Retreats

Whenever I teach a board seminar I'm always greeted with laughter and applause when I say, "Board planning retreats are the devil's spawn." Many participants in the board seminar have attended a two-day board retreat used to create a strategic plan for the organization. They have suffered through endless superficial discussions, board bullies who dominate the process, countless exhortations to "think outside the box," the mantra that 'we need to attract a younger audience' and the resulting anodyne plan in which no one really believes. They have been led to believe that planning retreats are 'good for them' but can't really understand why.

Let me be clear: I have nothing against boards taking time to meet together (and ideally with staff) in a remote location to discuss key issues and to allow for socializing. Normal board meetings do not afford the opportunity for substantial amounts of bonding. Establishing an esprit de corps amongst board and staff is very helpful.

But I do not think that a retreat is the appropriate place to write a plan. Why?

Because a good plan requires three key ingredients: data, time and creativity.

None of these three is fully available on a board retreat.

Too often, when data are not readily available, retreaters make assumptions about the correct information. By the end of the retreat, the assumption has become fact, at least in the minds of the participants. On too many occasions, these assumptions are incorrect and reflect conventional wisdom, which is often not very wise. Without proper data, a strong analytical base — a prerequisite for good planning — cannot be established.

Time is also a key planning requirement. One needs time to collect and assimilate data and to develop and test potential strategies. Some seemingly good ideas are eventually discarded after more thought; others are refined and amplified. I have yet to read a good plan whose central strategies were developed and evaluated in just 36 hours. When the entire planning process is shoe-horned into two days, the time required to do a good, competent job is simply not available.

And finally, a good plan requires creativity. How do we overcome a key weakness? How do we take best advantage of a central asset? Solving these challenges is difficult and requires creative thinking that cannot be assigned to a time slot between lunch and cocktails. Plans that are developed without the requisite amount of creative thought always sound like a simple listing of existing strategies, at best. At worst, they sound like a series of wishes: We will raise more money, we will sell more tickets, etc. And when the plan does not seem coherent or believable, board members who participated in the retreat feel like they wasted their time.

Although many board members might feel they can sit down for two days and create a plan for an arts organization, one must ask them, "Is that how you would do it for your own corporation?"

I can't imagine the answer would be yes.

DIVERSITY IN THE ARTS

For the past 20 years, I have had a great interest in the special benefits and challenges of arts organizations of color. Diverse arts organizations contribute greatly to our arts ecology. They provide new voices, new artists and new audiences.

But they also face special challenges, especially with respect to funding sources. The average Eurocentric arts organization receives approximately 60 percent of its contributions from individual donors; the average organization of color receives 6 percent of its contributions from individual donors. Arts organizations of color depend too heavily on government and foundation funding. These two funding sources are limited in number and are highly cyclical in their giving.

As a result, diverse organizations are typically limited in size and suffer disproportionately in bad economic times.

We need to protect our diverse organizations if we are going to protect the remarkable quilt that is our arts ecology.

Questions on Diversity

I have been spending a great deal of time thinking about the issue of diversity in the arts, specifically, the drive to diversify the programming and constituents of all arts organizations.

The more I consider this thorny issue, the less I am convinced that the arts world has worked hard enough to dissect the true costs, benefits and implications of recent diversity efforts.

Over the past 30 years, we were encouraged, primarily by foundation and government agencies, to become more diverse in every respect: We were asked to do works by minority artists, to bring diverse audiences to our theaters and to diversify our staffs and boards. To justify funding, the argument went, we had to demonstrate our commitment to our entire community.

Having spent a great deal of my career working with arts organizations of color, I am as committed as anyone to the diversity of our arts ecology. I do not believe that we can have a truly great artistic community if all segments of our society are not represented well.

But I do not think I believe anymore in forcing Eurocentric arts organizations to do diverse works or to put one minority on a board.

When large, white organizations produce minority works, they typically select the "low-hanging fruit," the most popular works by diverse artists featuring the most famous minority performers and directors. This almost invariably hurts the minority arts organizations in the neighborhood, most of which are small and underfunded and cannot afford to match the marketing clout or the casting glamour of their larger, white counterparts. How else to explain the reduced strength of American black theater companies over the past 20 years?

And when a single minority is placed on a board with no responsibility other than to represent a race, it does nothing to change the true mission, or audience base, of the organization. More is required. The Kennedy Center's Community Advisory Board, for example, is a non-fiduciary board that works actively to reach communities not adequately served by the Center.

My work has focused on teaching leaders of diverse arts organizations to find the resources needed to be strong advocates for and producers of the work of their communities. Arts organizations of color have been overly reliant on grants from foundations and government agencies, thereby limiting their size. We need to build the board strength of these vital groups and work with them to build individual donor bases that match their white counterparts. This is what the Alvin Ailey organization has done so brilliantly.

I would prefer to see great African American, Asian American, Latino and Native American arts organizations whose excellent work complements the excellent work of the large, white groups. And when a predominantly white organization does a major work by a minority artist, I would love to see it done in collaboration with an arts organization of color. When the Kennedy Center produced the entire August Wilson cycle, for example, we worked with Kenny Leon of True Colors Theatre Company.

I am not certain I am right. We need more discussion.

Our Annual Symposium for Arts Organizations of Color

Every March, a group of executives from 30 arts organizations of color gather at the Kennedy Center for an annual symposium. We created this group because I am particularly concerned that our diverse organizations are not strong enough, primarily because they do not raise enough money from individual donors. While the average white organization will raise some 60 percent of its donations from individuals, African American, Latino and Asian American organizations typically raise less than 10 percent from individuals. As a result, their budgets are limited to what can be raised from foundations and government agencies and a few corporations. Because their institutional donors are limited in number and are more cyclical than individual donors, arts organizations of color tend to be small and suffer disproportionately in a recession. Healthy arts organizations of color are needed if we are going to have the diversity of work, artists and training grounds needed to keep our artistic heritage the jewel it is. But these organizations are threatened by their small size and cyclical funding pattern. The Alvin Ailey organization is the only performing arts organization of color that has a budget exceeding $10 million a year.

This gathering is a family reunion of sorts. We have been working with these groups for eight years, and I have mentored several of them for up to 20 years.

For this reason, when we meet, we can get right to the point. There is no need to present pictures of the organizations that are overly rosy; I know their problems, personalities and predilections.

This year, we focused on ways to strengthen our boards. If building the number of individual donors is crucial for arts organizations of color, strengthening boards is a first step. Board members can play a central role in introducing their friends and associates to the organization. They can invite others to performances, exhibitions and galas. They can serve as ambassadors for the organization in the community, building excitement and interest in its work. An active, involved board is the foundation for the individual fundraising efforts of many arts organizations.

But too many arts organizations of color have boards that do not expect to play a major role in fundraising. They were formed as community boards and played a crucial role in the development of many diverse arts organizations. But as these organizations have grown, they need a different kind of board member, those with access to people of means who can broaden the sources of support.

So our seminar this year focused on why boards do not raise money and how to encourage them to do so. We examined how many board members are embarrassed about their organizations. They may love the mission of the group but are embarrassed by the financial condition, others on the board, typos in thank-you letters, etc. We discussed ways to make board members unembarrassed, especially through creative programming and institutional marketing efforts.

Once again, the groups surprised me with their creativity and determination. Many have already begun the process of building robust individual donor programs. Others are excited about beginning the process.

As always, at the conclusion of our annual meeting, I was left inspired, energized and a bit sad to see my friends go back to their home cities.

They are a remarkable group of arts leaders.

A Remarkable Class

I recently began teaching a series of arts management seminars for 10 grantees of the Ford Foundation. The foundation has committed $100 million over the next 10 years to support a new generation of arts spaces. According to the Foundation's website, "The initiative, Supporting Diverse Arts Spaces, will provide grant funds to support both new projects and the revitalization and expansion of existing arts spaces."

The Kennedy Center is responsible for delivering one element of the program: a mix of classes, web chats and site visits to help build the planning, marketing and fundraising skills of the grantees. I believe this is crucial since my fear for any arts organization building a new facility, or renovating an older one, is that so many resources and so much organizational focus is placed on the physical structure that the artistic and educational programming — the reasons for the building in the first place — can suffer.

We had our initial session in the Ellen Stewart Theatre at La MaMa Experimental Theatre Club in New York City. It was an incredibly exhilarating day. The 10 organizations are all vital, growing and important. They are led by amazing individuals who have both a deep sense of purpose and the maturity to appreciate the needs of growing and changing organizations.

Having this session at La MaMa, the oldest of the organizations, was particularly apt since my message to the group, as always, was that success in the arts was directly tied to strong, exciting, vital programming — just the kind of programming for which La MaMa has become famous. Maintaining this spirit of adventure and risk-taking is a challenge, especially in this economic environment.

The lesson of these 10 organizations is that success comes from the passionate disregard for those preaching to play it safe. The Hip-Hop Theater Festival has grown fast and furiously in 10 years, while Youth Speaks has created a new generation of young poets in San Francisco. Each of the other organizations — Ifetayo Cultural Arts Academy, Pa'i Foundation, Asian Arts Initiative, Ashé Cultural Center, First Peoples Fund, Alternate Roots and NALAC — provides innovative programming for diverse communities.

Each of the groups also faces challenges. Like most culturally-specific organizations (and rural and avant-garde organizations), individual donors play a very minor role in total funding. While the average white organization raises 60 percent or more of its contributions from individual donors, culturally-specific organizations typically raise less than 10 percent of their contributions from individual donors. These organizations are no exception.

This will be one of the central areas of focus for our teaching. If these organizations are going to grow to inhabit their new facilities fully, they will need stronger boards, better institutional marketing efforts and more individual donors.

I have no doubt that the remarkable leaders of these organizations will be able to meet these challenges. What they have already accomplished is deeply impressive. With the help of the Ford Foundation, and with some added capacity, these groups will become stable and visible role models for so many diverse arts organizations in this nation.

INTERNATIONAL

For well over a century, cultural exchange has been a central factor in the arts. Appreciating and collaborating with artists from abroad strengthens our work and introduces new sensibilities.

For just about as long, culture has been one tool in the arsenal of diplomats. Some countries, notably England and more recently China, have been highly sophisticated users of culture as a diplomatic tool.

At the Kennedy Center, we have focused on using culture to explain unfamiliar societies to our audiences in recent festivals of China, Japan, the Arab World and now India. We have also used arts management training as a way to foster international communication and cooperation.

I have no doubt that as 'the world shrinks,' international collaboration will become of greater importance to major arts organizations everywhere.

It is a topic that requires constant evaluation.

The Fundraising Challenge in Europe

For the past 10 years, my teaching abroad has focused on countries that are experiencing great political change and dramatic modifications in the arts ecology. I have taught in South Africa, Eastern Europe, the Arab World, Pakistan and China, for example.

But a recent teaching trip to Lisbon, Portugal, has me rethinking my strategy.

Lisbon is a beautiful city with a strong arts tradition. One has only to walk down virtually any street to appreciate the beautiful architecture and the appreciation of aesthetics.

But the arts world in Lisbon, like in other major European capitals, is in turmoil. How else can you explain that 450 people signed up for my class (which had seating capacity for 370)?

The current economic challenges in the world are forcing the government to reduce, sometimes radically, its support for arts organizations in the nation. This is clearly not a unique situation. Governments throughout Europe are now cutting arts subsidies, either gradually (France) or radically (England).

This is not a new problem, or news to me. But it was brought home so vividly during my class in Lisbon. I was introduced by the minister of culture, a passionate arts supporter and classical pianist of note, herself. She appreciates the challenges of both sides of the struggle; not only is she a minister and artist, but she has also turned around an important Portuguese orchestra.

The mood in the room was apprehensive and a bit hostile. Arts managers and artists were angry that the minister was not doing more to preserve their grants. And they did not know how to create other forms of income required to fill the gap left by reduced government support.

While it is easy to talk about ways to build donations from corporations and individuals, it isn't so easy to implement. Those arts managers brave enough to attempt to change their funding sources meet with mixed success on initial attempts. And it can be difficult to justify spending hours and hours to raise a few Euros when the government grant is virtually automatic (though arts managers there and elsewhere complain about the forms they must complete) and takes so little time to obtain.

But I remain convinced that some arts managers will be successful in building private philanthropy in Portugal and elsewhere. Already some are becoming successful. In England, for example, many major institutions can boast of highly sophisticated fundraising operations. It requires great discipline to keep at it, however. It takes courage to argue that a substantial portion of the budget will, one day, be financed by private contributions. And it takes a willingness to promote one's organization in a way that attracts contributions. This aggressive approach to marketing is counter-cultural.

It is likely to take one more generation of arts managers before private philanthropy is as common in Europe as it is in North America, if not as potent.

I think I will be spending far more time in Western Europe than I originally planned!

How Helpful Is Cultural Diplomacy?

For the last six years I have been obsessed with the concept of cultural diplomacy.

While other countries have been active exporters of their arts — China and Great Britain come to mind — the United States government has been reticent to invest in this form of diplomacy.

This was not always the case: Both American Ballet Theatre and the Alvin Ailey American Dance Theater added the word 'American' to their names at the request of the State Department about half a century ago when they were sent on government-sponsored international tours.

But while some American embassies abroad have been active in bringing American artists and arts groups to 'their' countries in recent years, this is still a very minor activity of the Department of State.

But does traditional cultural diplomacy work? Do we need state-supported tours by American performing arts groups when, without federal funding, so many of our performers and performing arts groups are appearing all over the world, when American architects are designing high-profile buildings internationally and when American artists are featured in the great museums? Does sending a symphony orchestra to play for a thousand of the most powerful people in the capital of another nation truly affect the way our nation is viewed? As the Obama administration tries to rebuild America's image abroad, do we need to send dance companies and theater companies abroad?

My response, not popular with my peers running arts organizations across the United States, is no.

Marketing only works (and cultural diplomacy *is* marketing) when it is frequently repeated. And it is simply too expensive to send orchestras and dance companies and theater groups to the same territory over and over again. And are we really influencing the citizens of a nation when we send performing groups to entertain the elite? Don't the elite come to the U.S. anyway? (And frankly, many people in foreign countries feel they get enough American culture via television, movies and popular music.)

But that does not mean that cultural diplomacy should be discarded. Rather, I believe we need to abandon traditional forms of cultural diplomacy in favor of a new approach.

The major problem facing arts organizations across the globe is a reduction in funding they are receiving from their governments. Outside of the United States, arts organizations in almost every country rely on government funding for the majority of their support. As governments find themselves unable to maintain this level of support, arts organizations are seeking new methods for finding funding.

Given our reliance on private funding, Americans have a great deal to teach abroad. We can teach how we build sponsorship by corporations and especially individuals. We can teach how we use marketing to expand the reach of our arts organizations. We can teach the importance of long-term program planning for building new sources of support.

I have been pursuing this form of cultural diplomacy for six years and have now taught arts managers in 60 countries.

These arts leaders now are attempting to support their organizations in new ways. They are grateful for the help they have received from the Kennedy Center, America's national cultural center. This gratitude extends to the governmental leaders of the nations in which we teach; it is not unusual for us to meet with mayors, ministers of culture and even presidents and prime ministers when we work abroad. They are all impressed that Americans care not just to export their own culture but to see to the health of arts organizations in their country and around the world. (And because we teach over a period of years, and build strong relationships in every country, the impact is far greater and longer-term than for any one concert.) The U.S. gains immense prestige and goodwill. And the cost is so small: one airline ticket and a hotel room.

While the Kennedy Center's international work is privately funded, maybe the State Department could support a program that allows other American arts organizations to teach abroad. (The money saved could be given to arts organizations to invest in programming, marketing and touring.)

Maybe this is a new way we can truly explain the value of a thoughtful, involved, generous democratic society across the globe?

My Visit to Croatia

I always enjoy visiting a new city and exploring its arts scene. Last month I was invited to teach in Zagreb, Croatia, home to one our DeVos Institute Summer Fellows, Zvonimir Dobrovic.

Zvonimir is a natural arts entrepreneur. At the young age of 32, he has already started two successful festivals that are supported by a mix of government and private contributions. I was there during Perforacije (Perforations), his new festival of Avant Garde theater, music and performance art. (His other festival, Queer Zagreb, is a gay arts festival he started at the age of 23 that will celebrate its 10th anniversary next Spring.)

Zvonimir's ability to attract government, corporate and individual support for his festivals is all the more remarkable given the prevailing arts funding environment in Croatia.

Like in most other countries in Europe, the huge majority of arts funding in Croatia comes from the government. To be sure, there is a vibrant group of small, adventuresome arts organizations that survive without government funding.

But the majority of arts organizations depend almost entirely on government grants.

It was fascinating to teach 200 arts leaders from Croatia and five surrounding Balkan countries, all with similar arts funding systems. The dependence of these arts managers on government funding influenced the way they approached their work. They could only budget for the amount the government gives them. They felt little or no power to find and spend additional resources. When I discussed long-term artistic planning, many of them felt like they had gone down the rabbit hole. How could they think of creating big, exciting arts projects five years from now when they were not certain of what their government grants would be? It took them one full day of class to begin to appreciate that they were the masters of their own destinies, that there were opportunities to find additional resources and that this would allow them to build their programming, reputations and ability to generate even more additional revenue.

Croatia is the rule in this world, not the exception. This is why people like Zvonimir, people who do not feel bounded by the grants they receive from their own governments, are so important. They serve as role models for their communities.

If a 23-year-old, young man can develop the resources to support a gay festival, then more experienced arts managers should be able to find the resources for opera, ballet and theater.

Many people I met in Croatia are skeptical that private philanthropy can thrive there. I had the honor to meet with the hugely popular president of Croatia, Ivo Josipovic, a musician, composer and arts manager. He was clear on the need to build new sources of arts funding; his country, and most others, simply cannot maintain the levels of funding needed to support all domestic arts organizations. But he also understood that it would be a challenge to build a large base of private support. We discussed the various actions the government could take to encourage corporate and individual giving to the arts. His advisors were far more skeptical than he was about the ability to create a culture of philanthropy in Croatia.

I disagreed, of course, and presented Zvonimir Dobrovic as Exhibit A.

My Visit to Venice

I had the good fortune this summer to visit Venice, Italy, one of the wonders of this world. Wandering through the canals and alleys of this amazing city, I happened upon La Fenice, the major opera house in Venice, and was surprised that a tour was available in the depths of August.

La Fenice is most appropriately named; its name means "The Phoenix." Several times in its history it has been destroyed by fire, most recently in 1996, and has reemerged more beautiful than before.

La Fenice has been one of the most important opera houses for over two centuries. Donizetti, Bellini and numerous other composers were commissioned to write operas for this amazing house. Verdi alone wrote *Attila*, *Rigoletto*, *La Traviata* and *Simon Boccanegra* for La Fenice!

Walking into its astonishing, ornate, albeit intimate, hall today, one cannot help but be impressed by the dedication of those who saw to the most recent reconstruction efforts. Every detail has been attended to, every element of the reconstruction seems as fresh today as it did seven years ago when it reopened. The theater literally takes one's breath away.

I was fortunate to visit La Fenice with a friend who had never been in an opera house before, let alone seen an opera. He has visited many impersonal, modern venues for pop concerts and could not believe what a special place this was. He left our tour wanting to attend an opera performance as soon as possible.

My friend was drawn to opera because of his visit to La Fenice. My entry into the performing arts came over 50 years ago in a very different but equally riveting way. My parents took my brother, my sister and me to see *The Music Man* at the Majestic Theatre on Broadway, starring the amazing Barbara Cook as Marian the Librarian. I was dazzled by the theater, the curtain, the orchestra and the buzz of the audience. And when Miss Cook sang *Goodnight My Someone* on the porch of her home, we could suddenly see through the walls of the house into its interior. I didn't know about scrims at the time. I only knew this was truly a magical moment in my life. I knew I would be spending much of my life trying to experience this magic again. And I have.

I think we forget about the impression that a beautiful theater can create. Bringing newcomers, especially children, to a glorious theater and allowing them to enjoy the heady cocktail of art and architecture is certainly one important way to build our audiences. In an era when so much of what we experience comes to us via electronic transmission, when we listen to iPods, talk on iPhones, watch performances on television and play on our laptop computers, we forego the pleasure, the excitement and the mystery of the live performance in the magical theater. While electronics offer an efficient way to introduce people to the arts, I dare say they are not nearly as effective as experiencing the real thing in a real theater.

Especially if the theater is as stunning as La Fenice or the performers are as astonishing as Barbara Cook.

My Trip to Cape Town

If you have never been to Cape Town — especially during summertime there — you are missing out on one of the world's great cities. It is a far trip from most places on earth; it takes 20 or more hours to get there from Washington, D.C. But it is worth every minute of the journey.

Table Mountain, wine country, the beach and a vibrant arts culture are all to be enjoyed. The *a cappella* singing, opera and ballet, vivid theater productions and dynamic visual arts are abundant. A visit to Robbin Island, where Nelson Mandela was incarcerated, reminds us in a most moving fashion of the country's ugly history in the 20th century and the way it is rebuilding its economy and its spirit in this one.

I have been coming to Cape Town, and other South African cities, to teach arts management for over 15 years. The city has never seemed so vibrant. This June and July, the World Cup of Soccer will be hosted in South Africa, with eight of the matches taking place in a new stadium in Cape Town. The city has improved infrastructure and tourist services, including hotels, roads, restaurants and the airport to serve the hundreds of thousands of visitors who are expected.

In my teaching sessions, one unfortunate fact emerged: For most South Africans, the planning for the World Cup ends with the final match on July 11. The world ends the next day.

This has an effect on all members of the community, including the arts community. Everyone is building for this June and July; I did not hear of many plans for arts programming for 2011 or beyond.

It is this type of boom and bust planning that decimates arts organizations, especially those in areas where the arts have yet to create a firm funding infrastructure.

So many arts groups are thriving now. They are hiring staff, adding performances, building on the excitement and the economic stimulation caused by this greatest of world sporting events (sorry, Super Bowl).

But what happens the following month or year? Do all of the funders simply turn their attention away from the arts and to other ventures? Must the arts world retreat after its most successful year ever?

Good artistic planning extends for years. The most successful arts organizations, from every perspective, will be those that have a great plan for this year but equally exciting programs planned for 2011, 2012 and beyond. They will be the ones that build consistently on the foundation established this year. They will keep their sponsors, build their audiences, enhance reputations and grow in a smoother and more sustainable manner.

At this point, there appears to be little that is special planned for Cape Town in the hangover year of 2011. Couldn't the arts fill this void? Isn't this an opportunity to become a more vital part of the local and national agenda?

I imagine this is not a problem unique to arts organizations or to Cape Town. But it is frustrating nonetheless in this amazing city.

Our Visit to Japan

The Kennedy Center is fortunate to have the support of our International Committee on the Arts, a group of patrons from many countries who help to underwrite our international programming. This programming includes both the presentations of international artists and festivals at the Center and the training we offer to arts managers around the world.

Each year, the committee holds a summit in a foreign country. This meeting allows us to discuss our international strategy, our current projects and the opportunities we see for the future. We also have an opportunity to experience the culture, history and, of course, food of the host nation. In past years, summits were held in Beijing, St. Petersburg, Rome, Paris, London and Buenos Aires. Next year we will visit Cape Town, South Africa.

This year the committee met for one stimulating week in Tokyo and Kyoto. Our business meetings focused on our summer fellowship program that will bring 42 arts managers from 28 different nations to the Center this summer. The members of the committee were particularly moved by a letter from a summer fellow from Nigeria who wrote of the murder and rape of hundreds in his city and the importance of art for the healing of his community. We also reviewed the numerous international presentations we are hosting at the Center this season and next, including this season's VSA International Festival and next season's festival of India.

The committee members also toured through each city visiting temples, museums, private art collections and historical monuments. We even attended the national championship sumo wrestling matches and the astonishing Tokyo fish market.

One of the highlights of each of these summits is an event that honors important artists from the host country. Previous honorees have included Valery Gergiev, Paloma Herrera, Julio Bocca, Trevor Nunn, Olivia de Havilland and Judi Dench. This year we honored four astonishing artists: architect Tadao Ando, violinist Midori, Kabuki actor Kanzaburo Nakamura and director Yukio Ninagawa.

What made this event special, apart from the remarkable artistry of each of the honorees, was that all four had participated in Kennedy Center programming. Kanzaburo Nakamura, who comes from a remarkably distinguished line of Kabuki actors, performed at the Center decades ago. Midori has been a frequent soloist with the National Symphony Orchestra and in recital. And both Tadao Ando and Yukio Ninagawa participated in our *JAPAN: culture + hyperculture* festival two years ago.

Because all four honorees had a relationship to the Kennedy Center, there was a lovely sense of family that developed that evening. The honorees were both gracious and self-effacing during their remarks. They all had great memories of working at the Center and appreciated the need for additional cultural exchange opportunities.

Needless to say, the members of our International Committee left Japan with a deep appreciation for the beauty and richness of Japanese culture and new motivation to continue to support the work the Kennedy Center does to use arts to educate our audiences about other people.

To Build or Not to Build

I was fortunate to be invited to attend a symposium offered by the Young Arab Theatre Fund in Alexandria, Egypt.

This group facilitates discussions amongst Arab artists and arts managers. This biannual symposium presents one of the few networking opportunities for Arab arts leaders.

I was asked to present a half-day workshop on arts management issues.

I discussed the model for artistic and financial success that I suggest to all arts organizations, regardless of location: strong artistic planning leading to aggressive marketing, leading to focused fundraising, leading to more resources, leading to better art, and on and on.

As usual, when I teach in any country where the arts funding infrastructure is either nascent or changing (e.g. Pakistan, Eastern Europe, South America), there was particular concern about the ability to plan art years in advance.

The political and economic challenges of the region make planning three, four or even five years in advance seem downright silly. Yet I still believe an arts organization in Damascus, Cairo or Ramallah is more likely to achieve its goals if it plans years in advance, recognizing that plans can change.

As always, there were a few (young) participants who 'got it.' They were not yet jaded or beaten down by the challenges of their environment.

But one topic I discussed became truly controversial: the 'right' time for an arts organization to commit to its own facility. I have always believed that an arts organization that tries to build or renovate a facility before it is ready ends up diverting its focus from its mission (producing great art and education) to building the facility. This can lead to a reduction in annual fundraising, less interesting or smaller programs and a loss of audience and community support.

The Alvin Ailey organization provides a great example of how to do it right. Even though the organization was stabilized in 1993, it took another decade before it embarked on its building campaign. By that time, it was ready to switch some of its focus to this effort because its annual efforts were so mature and strong.

My audience in Alexandria did not agree with me. One very smart and sophisticated manager from Lebanon took particular exception with my remarks. She believed that having a facility made a statement about the importance and permanence of the arts. She believed that without a facility an arts organization would appear marginal. She believed that in her country, with a highly unstable political situation, that it was crucial that the arts build a physical infrastructure.

Her arguments are strong and compelling. But I can't help worrying that if arts organizations, in Lebanon, Buenos Aires or Dubuque, build facilities (or sign long-term leases and renovate spaces) before they have the fiscal wherewithal to maintain the quality of their programming, they may not be able to sustain themselves and grow in a consistent manner.

Our Summer Fellows

Last week a new class of summer fellows arrived at the Kennedy Center for a four-week session. The summer fellows program brings arts managers from nations around the world to the Kennedy Center. The fellows come for three years in a row to study fundraising, marketing, financial management and planning. The program is a three-year program because we want our students to learn, to go home and experiment, to come back and learn some more and so forth. Simply giving them some information and sending them on their way would not be sufficient.

Our summer fellows are smart, ambitious and determined to make a difference in their home countries. They are extraordinary ambassadors for their nations. But virtually all of them live in countries where there is little or no access to arts management training. They have learned to manage their organizations on their own.

Patrick-Jude Oteh, from Jos, Nigeria, runs a theater company that has not only to cope with a dearth of donors, the difficulty of building an audience, and the challenges of creating a board, but he does it while insurgents are killing and raping hundreds of people in his town.

Zvonimir Dubrovik, just 29 years old, successfully created and maintained for seven years a substantial gay arts festival in Zagreb, Croatia. While developing this project successfully, he also created a new contemporary arts festival and is about to develop a project in New York City.

Noora Baker runs a modern dance company in Ramallah, Palestine, and Tanya Surtees an avant-garde theater company in Cape Town, South Africa, that mixes deaf and hearing actors.

There are 41 such stories this summer, as we welcome, for the first time, a first-year class and returning second- and third-year students. Now in its steady state, the summer institute will allow each summer fellow to interact with five classes, or some 75 international arts managers, over the three-year course. This 'United Nations of arts management' is creating a network of well-trained arts entrepreneurs who are certain to shape the arts world for decades to come.

And working on an ongoing basis with these immensely talented individuals also confirms our belief that cultural diplomacy is about building long-term relationships. We build relationships with these amazing individuals who will truly lead their nations in the years to come. The art they produce will help shape the minds of the citizens of their countries. The relationships we form, that continue long after the fellowship is over, can only help America rebuild its image abroad. The image created of American generosity (our fellows all receive full scholarships), expertise and belief that the health of the arts world anywhere depends on the health of arts organizations everywhere must certainly make an impact.

As our happy band of international arts leaders celebrates July Fourth together, watching fireworks and sharing a picnic, one develops great hope not just for the world of the arts but for the world itself.

ARTS MANAGEMENT

Virtually everything I write is meant to provide information and ideas to arts managers. But there are several columns that are specifically aimed at this group of arts leaders.

Arts managers are unified in their determination to provide great art and arts education to their communities. But we face a long list of serious challenges that is not getting any shorter.

Our audiences and donor bases are aging, public money for art and arts education is shrinking, alternative forms of entertainment are cannibalizing our audiences and our board members are not educated about the needs of our institutions.

There are also very few places for us to look for personal and professional counseling as we combat these difficult problems.

I try to write often about these issues in an effort to provide some level of support, if only second-hand.

And if all else fails, we can always stage primal scream day!

The Biggest Problem Facing the Arts

This week we will welcome 10 new arts management fellows to the Kennedy Center. These talented young people will spend an academic year with us studying the many elements of arts management, including planning, marketing, programming and fundraising. They will work on major projects in our numerous departments and participate in high-level meetings with senior staff, donors and board members.

This fellowship program, now in its ninth year, is but one project of the Kennedy Center Arts Management Institute. We also have developed programs for arts organizations of color, international arts managers, arts managers in Washington D.C., New York City and the Midwest, and for the training of board members of arts organizations.

Why does the Kennedy Center devote so many resources to these programs? Because the central problem facing the arts today is not a lack of flute players, choreographers, actors or painters. The main challenge the arts world must address is the lack of a large, trained corps of managers who know how to find resources, attract audiences and other constituents and provide support to our artists.

Arts management is a young field. While wonderful impresarios have operated for centuries, serious codification of the rules of arts management began fewer than 50 years ago. And while we have a number of academic programs offered by universities across the nation, there are simply not enough of them, and several are too academic in their approach. Arts management, after all, is a practical field, like medicine, and must be taught through real-time, real-world experiences.

There are, of course, a large number of wonderfully talented arts leaders; many of them were self-taught, others learned from a mentor. But there are not enough of these excellent leaders to serve our many arts organizations. Smaller arts organizations have a particular challenge with management. All too often, when managers distinguish themselves in small organizations, they are wooed away by larger, more prestigious institutions that can afford to pay higher salaries. The small organizations, which enjoyed a period of great entrepreneurship and growth, find themselves unable to attract equally talented replacements.

Arts leaders in the next decades will face radical changes in technology, a generation of potential audience members who did not participate in the arts at school, ticket prices that disenfranchise whole blocks of our population and online activities that provide serious competition for audiences. If the arts are going to survive this period of transition, we need to invest far more heavily in arts management than we have in the past.

Strong, trained, talented arts administrators will find solutions to this growing list of problems. They will help their organizations adapt and thrive, and they will provide the support artists need to do their work.

But I fear that unless we address the arts management challenge, too many arts organizations will fail to find proper solutions to these challenges, and we will see too many talented artists without the resources they deserve and too many communities without access to the arts and arts education.

New Season Anxiety

The new arts season begins this month for many arts organizations. For me the start of a season holds a mixture of excitement and dread, not unlike the feeling of a roller coaster hitting its zenith with a precipitous drop to come.

I am terribly excited by the slate of projects we have spent years planning. I know some of them will be remarkable and potent, fulfilling my fondest wishes. I cannot tell you at this point which projects will be successful, but I am confident that the successes will justify the failures.

I am scared to death, however, that we will not have the resources to pay for these projects. Will we sell the number of tickets we expect? Will our fundraising efforts bear enough fruit?

I don't think I am unique in this mix of feelings. My guess is that thousands of other arts managers are also excited and scared this month.

It is interesting to compare this set of feelings to those of someone from the for-profit sector, the members of our boards, for example. As a new fiscal year dawns for a corporation, I am sure senior executives have the same concerns we do about success. Will sales meet expectations? Will costs be controlled? Will new products succeed or fail?

But the reward structure is so different in the for-profit and the not-for-profit sectors. If we are successful in the arts, we are proud of the work we have created and relieved that we generated the resources to pay ourselves, our artists and staff members. We are satisfied (thrilled?) with balanced budgets that pay this year's expenses but provide no resources for the future.

If a corporate executive is successful, huge personal financial gain is earned, the corporation builds a cushion against future failure and the ability to raise capital increases.

But arts executives never feel this new season anxiety let up. Those of us who have been in this field for decades are just as threatened this year as we were 10 years ago. Our organizations don't build large cushions since we don't earn large surpluses, and we don't earn huge bonuses even if the work we produce is wonderful and our budgets are balanced.

No wonder our board members do not appreciate our elevated stress levels at the start of a season. I have been told more times than I can count, "Why are you scared? After all, you have been so successful for years."

And no wonder so many great arts executives leave the field prematurely.

It is simply too scary. And at some point the accumulation of fear outweighs the excitement about the next production.

The only antidote I have found is to plan very well and to raise money for large projects years in advance. At least feeling prepared and having some money raised in advance reduce the stress I feel at the inception of a new season. But I would be lying if I suggested I am not having sleepless nights this month.

My Prescription for Summer

Every June I make the same recommendation to my students: Use the summer months to plan for the future of your organizations but also, and vitally, to replenish yourselves for the year ahead.

During the height of the season, it is difficult, if not impossible, for many arts executives to do comprehensive, thoughtful long-term planning. Leaders of smaller arts organizations especially have trouble finding enough time to clear their minds and schedules of day-to-day challenges and to think more creatively and openly about the future of their organizations. Without this planning time, however, arts organizations are in danger of doing similar things every year, failing to solve central challenges and looking boring to audiences and donors. It is the surprising project that builds institutional image, not the routine.

The summer months, when most arts organizations are doing a minimum of producing (or the winter months for summer festivals), provide the perfect time for reflection. Just how good is our programming and how do we make it better? What kinds of projects do we dream of producing? How can we make this happen? How can we create the resources required and when might we find these resources? How can I build the image for excellence this organization needs to attract strong new board members, motivate those board members we have and increase audience size at a reasonable cost? What sources of funding have we failed to energize and how can we do so in the future? What worked especially well this past season? What could have been substantially better? Why?

These questions and many others demand thoughtful analysis and creative thinking. The answers cannot be rushed, and neither conventional wisdom nor superficial responses are helpful. The summer months, when things are less hectic, are the perfect time to reflect, respond and begin implementation.

But the summer months are also the time when we must replenish our souls.

We need to get enough sleep, for sure, but sleep is not really the central answer for the tired arts executive. We need to also divert our attentions to non-work activities. A true vacation is not necessarily a trip to Paris or a week at the beach. A vacation is anything that allows your mind to refocus on other interests and endeavors.

For some of us this can mean learning a new language, reading important books or spending relaxed time with friends and family. Taking time away from obsessing about our work is essential if we are to return in the Fall with renewed vigor and energy and excitement.

All arts leaders have been through a terribly difficult two-year period. But our roles demand that we not let our fatigue affect the way we lead. If we cannot return in September filled with excitement for the year ahead and optimism that our plans will help bring our organizations to a new level, we have no hope that our boards, staffs, artists and donors will approach the new season with anything but ennui.

Ignore this prescription for summer at your own peril!

A Lasting Legacy of Recession

One of the legacies of the lengthy recession we appear to be leaving behind us is that arts leaders are exhausted.

I have spoken with thousands of arts managers over the past six months, and it is astonishing how many are considering leaving their positions in the relatively near future.

Very few of them are departing for wonderful new opportunities with other arts organizations. The vast majority are planning to leave their jobs with no new position on the horizon.

These managers are so tired of struggling to create interesting programming while balancing the budget and appeasing their (nervous) boards that they feel they need a break. For the past two years, they have felt pressured by both passionate artists who want to do their work regardless of the economic situation and conservative board members, many of whose own companies are in trouble. The challenge of appeasing both at the same time has been overwhelming.

That so many arts leaders are considering leaving their jobs (or the profession) at the same time cannot be good for the arts. These managers possess a wealth of experience and talent that will not be easily replaced. (One of the challenges of the arts is that few organizations have 'seconds in command' who are prepared to run an organization after the current leader departs. While corporations often have people ready to step into the leader's position, few arts organizations have the resources required to fund a 'number two.')

Many board members, tired and frustrated as well after the past two difficult years, harbor the belief that their organizations would benefit from new managerial blood. They believe that the current managers did not have the skills required to deal with the economic downturn, did not cut budgets quickly enough or deeply enough, were not able to market the organization effectively and did inadequate fundraising.

The truth is there is not a wealth of experienced arts managers waiting to take these leadership positions. Ironically, board members only realize this after the current leader departs and they face a negligible pool of willing and able applicants. Too often, board members opt for a financial person from the for-profit sector, hoping their skills and discipline will help solve the organization's financial problems. (Of course, these board members are forgetting that financial people measure problems; they rarely solve them!)

I hope a massive hiring effort is not required in the coming year. That as the season comes to a close, these exhausted managers will use the summer to replenish themselves, to regain their excitement for their work and their passion for arts management. That many, if not most, of them will reconsider their plans and remain with the organizations that need them.

And I hope that board members will remember that the arts managers they employ have been through two of the most difficult years in their lives, and they need and deserve support, encouragement and gratitude.

A Fundamental Problem with Our Arts Ecology

Over the last year I have noticed a change in the reactions by major donors, especially foundations, to serious fiscal problems experienced by important arts organizations.

In the past, if an organization with a history of major contributions to the field became seriously ill, donors would rally and work to shore up the organization until it could clean house, strengthen its board and hire new staff leadership. This was not always a clean or easy process, but arts organizations with strong reputations were not allowed to go out of business without a fight.

There seemed to be a belief that organizations with important histories of artistic excellence, or organizations that were leaders in communities of color, should be saved and given a second (or third) chance to create stability. I was involved in such turnarounds at the Alvin Ailey American Dance Theater and American Ballet Theatre in the 1990s. I could not have saved these institutions without the tremendous support of important funders. The Ford Foundation, for example, played a key role in saving Ailey, and the Mellon Foundation was instrumental in the turnaround at ABT.

During this recession, however, funders have taken a harder tone. "When there are well run organizations that are struggling to replace donors who have evaporated, why support those that have poor management, weak boards, and unrealistic plans and budgets," the funding community seems to be suggesting.

It is hard to argue with this logic, but it is also dangerous not to. The line between sickness and health is a slim one in the arts. It can take one competent staff leader or a few energized board members to initiate the process of fixing a troubled arts organization.

Letting organizations like the Baltimore Opera, Charleston Symphony or the Las Vegas Art Museum close comes at a huge cost to their communities. And it is especially sad when they are allowed to disband when their deficits are modest compared to their histories of service.

It seems disingenuous for major funders to chastise or ignore organizations with poor management when these same funders have avoided funding programs to improve the quality of arts managers. We spend billions of dollars to train singers, dancers and actors, and insignificant amounts to train the people who employ them.

I have said it before and I will continue to say it: The biggest problem we face in the arts is a lack of trained arts managers and board members. One can trace the demise of virtually every bankrupt arts organization to a lack of competent staff and/or board leadership. There are many, well-managed arts organizations that are surviving this recession. It is not easy for any arts manager, but those with knowledge and skill are seeing their organizations through this most challenging environment.

Until the funding community addresses this issue of arts management training, they will continue to be faced with organizations of artistic and educational merit that are going to ask for emergency funding and be forced to close if they do not receive it.

Isn't it time to discuss this fundamental problem in our arts ecology?

Artistic Directors vs. Executive Directors

Over the last several weeks I have been visiting cities across the nation, discussing ways to address the current economic crisis. Amidst all of the pain, fear and serious discussion, one area of conversation always gets a laugh: the way to reduce tension between artistic directors and executive leadership.

I always compare the relationship between these two staff heads to that between a naughty child (artistic director) and an angry parent (executive director). The naughty child is always asking for "More, more, more!" and the angry parent says "No! No! No! We can't afford it." The lack of trust that develops between the two people who are meant to act as a team is ineffective at best and crippling at worst.

I appreciate the fears of the executive director; I have been one for 24 years. When one does not know where the money will come from to pay artists, staff, production costs, rent, etc., one hopes to trim every expense possible. Good executive directors appreciate that they cannot fulfill the wishes of the artistic director if they do not have the money to do so, and in the current economic environment, anything extra seems impossible.

But the truth is that the only reason the executive director has a job is to fulfill the wishes of the artistic director. And good artistic directors always have a wish list because they want to expand the boundaries of the organization and to consistently produce great art. I have yet to see the mission of a not-for-profit arts organization that says, "Our goal is to have a good balance sheet and income statement." (Actually I once read the mission statement of a not-for-profit arts organization that said only, "Our goal is to have a balanced budget." Clearly this organization did not aspire to very much. They could best fulfill this mission by doing nothing!)

I find that it is easiest to meet the needs of the artists while maintaining fiscal stability by developing a long-term artistic plan for the organization. I believe there are many reasons to plan one's productions or exhibitions three, four or even five years in advance, including the ability to satisfy the artistic goals of the institution in an affordable manner.

I always make a simple chart that shows the major artistic and educational programs planned for each of the next five years. This plan includes all the items on my artistic director's wish list. I array these items in a way that makes me confident that I can fulfill this contract with my artistic director. I know that if I have several years to raise the funds, form a joint venture, organize a tour or create a marketing campaign required for a larger project, I am most likely to be able to accomplish what is necessary.

I have yet to find an artistic director who wants everything immediately. In fact, most artistic directors are so used to being told no for many of the things they ask, that if one can provide a plan for accomplishing all they desire, they become far more confident that the executive director is on their side and a new, far better relationship between them can be formed.

The Art of Celebration

One of the things arts managers very often forget to do is to celebrate success. It is easy in the current economic climate, when we are all struggling to make ends meet, to ignore this vital element of good leadership. But I would argue that this is the time we need to celebrate victory most of all.

All members of our organizational 'families' need the motivation and inspiration that come from celebrating the victories our organization enjoys. Mounting a great production, increasing enrollment in an education program, securing a major foundation gift or simply surviving another fiscal year, all demand celebration.

We must take the time to gather our artists, educators, board members, volunteers and staff and celebrate those activities that went well and to thank the many participants who worked so hard to make the project possible.

At a time when so many board members are fearful and pessimistic, when staff members are exhausted from coping with two years of recession, and when artists question whether the institution has it priorities in place, and when there does not seem to be an end in sight to the fiscal challenges we face, it is essential to take time to acknowledge that we are still vibrant and important organizations making progress and contributions to our communities.

Celebrations can take the form of a simple e-mail to all 'family' members, an informal gathering, picnic or trip to an amusement park, or a more formal meeting or dinner where successes are detailed and appreciation expressed. The esprit de corps that is established at these events can help carry participants through the next set of challenges and crises. And the public recognition that good work has been accomplished can ease tensions that easily arise between board and staff and between executive and artistic staffs during difficult years.

Of course one must be careful. One does not want to over-hype minor successes nor does one want to leave the impression that the organization is unaware of larger challenges and problems it faces. Some will argue that when staff members are facing furloughs or salary freezes, or cuts are being made to artistic or educational programming, it is uncomfortable to have a party or to celebrate a new grant.

But the key is to place the victory in context of the overall plan for the organization.

If the organization has devised a strategy to move it from its current position to a new, more secure place of higher achievement, celebrating successes along the way confirms that the strategy is working. This can encourage all participants, especially board members and donors, to continue their support.

Managing an arts organization successfully is, in large measure, a challenge in psychology. We ask so many things from so many people, many of whom are either not compensated or undercompensated for their participation.

Celebrating institutional successes in visible ways encourages every participant to continue to work to implement the strategic plan. This is an inexpensive, joyful way to encourage strategy implementation.

The DeVos Institute of Arts Management

Pardon me while I celebrate a landmark commitment to my pet project. Betsy and Dick DeVos of Grand Rapids, Michigan, have committed $22.5 million to supporting our arts management institute at the Kennedy Center, which has now been renamed the DeVos Institute of Arts Management at the Kennedy Center.

This pledge, a mix of operating and endowment funds, gives permanence to a project we initiated in 2001 with our Fellowship Program.

It must be the largest gift ever for arts management training in the United States or abroad, acknowledgment of the perceived importance of arts management training.

I have been lobbying for more attention for arts management training since the early 1990s. It has been abundantly clear to me that we spend a disproportionate share of professional arts training on performers and creators. In fact, billions of dollars are spent educating dancers, singers, pianists and actors. We spend a pittance on training the people who will employ them, who will find resources to support their work and will attract their audiences.

Many universities have started arts management programs over the past 30 years. I taught in the NYU Masters program for six years. These programs have provided a foundation of arts management knowledge for young arts managers, but they are not sufficient to meet our arts management training needs. We have thousands of managers without sufficient training at senior levels of many of our arts institutions. These hardworking, talented individuals are not likely to return to school for a postgraduate degree at this point in their careers.

We need opportunities for practicing arts managers to hone their craft, and we need laboratories that give them a chance to practice what they learn in the classroom. Just as no one would hire a doctor who had only learned by reading a book to operate on them, arts mangers need more than a classroom education.

That is why we started our arts management institute at the Kennedy Center. We train mid-career arts executives in the U.S. and around the world through a coordinated series of year-long fellowships for American arts managers, summer fellowships for international students, capacity-building seminars in cities throughout the United States, board seminars, and online resources on artsmanager.org.

And we offer a real, working arts organization in which our students and young professionals can get practical training.

Until we received this grant from the DeVoses, the institute felt fragile. Even though we have received millions of dollars of grants from numerous funders over the past several years to create training programs, I was worried that the programming was far too dependent on me. This gift gives a true sense of permanence to the institute; it provides the funding needed to build a cadre of trained mentors and the teaching materials required for our classes.

I am so grateful to Betsy and Dick DeVos and am so pleased that our institute now bears their name.

The Evolution of Boards

As I travel around the country talking about the problems facing arts organizations during this recession, there is one topic that gets consistent and passionate attention: the role of the board.

Most board members I meet are scared and frustrated, and most staff members believe their board members are not being as generous or as helpful as they should be during this crisis.

I believe there is a common mistaken notion that board members are *responsible* for generating the contributed revenue needed by an organization. While it is true that boards are responsible for approving fundraising plans and budgets, I do not think that it is realistic to ask a group of volunteers to take full responsibility for generating contributed funds. I have always felt it was my job, as a staff leader, to motivate my board to be helpful but that ultimately the final responsibility lies with me.

How does one get board members to raise funds? I believe the best method is to get each board member to adopt a project. This can be a performance or educational program, a gala or a marketing campaign. (Rarely does a board member embrace every program of an organization.) By allowing them to delve into a project, meet the artists, come to rehearsals, etc, they build an allegiance to that project. This, in turn, motivates them to get their friends and associates to invest in the program's success.

But this technique only works if the board members have the connections they need to be helpful and are willing to use them.

Many arts board members simply do not have connections necessary for helping the organization. These board members may have passion for the organization but cannot be helpful with fundraising. This is not typically a problem when an organization is young. But as it matures, the role of board members must change. Board members of young organizations frequently act as staff, doing the bookkeeping, the marketing and even sewing the costumes. As the organization matures, the nature of the board members must change as well. No longer does the board have to do the bookkeeping; but they must have access to funds needed to support the larger infrastructure.

This means that boards must mature and change as organizations do. This is the responsibility of the Nominating (or Governance) Committee, to evaluate what the board should 'look like' and how it must change over time.

At the same time, staff leaders must make sure the programming and institutional marketing are so strong that board members are excited about inviting their friends and do not suffer from 'board embarrassment syndrome,' the fear that their friends and associates may not enjoy becoming involved.

When the board attends to its membership and the staff creates exciting programming and strong marketing campaigns, any arts organization can enjoy a steady and developing involvement of its board in its success.

The Importance of Midpoint Corrections

January represents the midpoint in the season for many United States arts organizations. By this point, many of us know whether the year is progressing as we had expected when we developed the budget for the year.

For too many of us, the news this season isn't good. A major grant may have been lost, a production may have died at the box office or a project went wildly over budget. For most organizations, at least one element of the fundraising campaign is not meeting target. At this rate, many arts organizations are headed for a serious deficit for the fiscal year.

So what do we do?

One thing we cannot do is 'hope' that things get better. They rarely do by themselves.

Too many arts managers simply accept the fact that this season is not going well and believe that next year will be better. (And a good percentage of these managers base next year's budget on this year's budget, rather than this year's actual results; this makes next year's budget even more difficult to achieve.) These managers are often so busy planning for next year they forget that there is work to be done to salvage this year.

This month we must split our focus. Of course we must plan for the season ahead, develop our subscription brochures and finish (start?) our budget for next season.

But we must also change course midstream for this season if the results are not good enough. We must cut budgets and accelerate the search for new contributions and new audience members. If we wait until spring, it will be too late to make meaningful budget cuts and to implement revenue-enhancement programs.

Because I talk publicly so often about not cutting programming or marketing in the face of fiscal challenges, some people believe that I don't cut budgets at all. This is, of course, untrue, as my staff will readily attest. Virtually every year, somewhere from December to February, I cut the budget if I see that revenue is not what we had expected or costs have gotten out of control.

We cannot wait for our boards to demand cuts; we have to make them ourselves.

I, personally, cannot sleep when I have not figured out how to balance my budget. This is not a happy way to live, but it is a healthy one for the organizations I manage.

Thinning Out the Field

I have heard from so many people over the past two years that this might be the time to 'thin out the field' of arts organizations. The argument goes that there are more organizations than can be supported by the existing group of donors in a given community. If the weaker organizations either closed or merged with stronger organizations, competition for dollars would be reduced and the entire field would be healthier.

I do not agree with this prescription for a number of reasons.

First, it assumes that there is some fixed level of donors and donations in any city or town. I do not believe this is true. I believe that there is an endless supply of donors if the art is exciting enough and the marketing is potent enough. It is true that in many cities, there is a group of donors who have been so loyal and generous to the arts that every arts group solicits these donors first. But an organization that fails to expand its donor base beyond these loyal few does so at its own peril. Donors die, move away and change giving interests. And if a few donors are always the 'go-to people' when money must be raised, they are more likely to suffer from donor fatigue. Every arts community must work diligently to engage new donors.

It also assumes that existing donors will happily shift their allegiance from one (now defunct) organization to another. This has not always been my experience. With the exception of foundations, which are required by law to give out donations each year, donors do not have to keep giving. In fact, many donors are attracted to the specific mission of a given arts organization. If that organization closes its doors, its donors may stop giving to the arts entirely.

And finally, this approach assumes that the strongest arts organizations, in terms of fiscal health, should survive. I am more interested in making artistically strong arts organizations more stable than assuring an easier playing field for financially strong organizations. I would rather spend time and resources training the board and staff leaders of challenged organizations that produce interesting work to find new resources than to see them evaporate so that larger organizations (whose art may not be very interesting after all) can have an easier time of it. I fear that the diverse voices that characterize the most potent arts ecologies would be silenced if only the 'strong' organizations remained.

Why do people who suggest thinning out the field always come from larger, stronger organizations after all? I have yet to hear someone attached to a small, weak organization suggesting the thinning out strategy!

Maybe if boards, working with the staff leadership, spent more time planning strong fundraising efforts rather than demanding that budgets be cut our arts organizations would be healthier.

Perhaps we need to stop thinking about ways to make it easier at the expense of others and start thinking about ways to make our work more interesting to a wider set of audience members and donors.

And maybe we need to remember that while a greater range of arts organizations might make for more competition, it also makes for a far more interesting arts environment.

Conventional Wisdom

I was asked an interesting question on my "Arts in Crisis" tour stop in Phoenix: Is there conventional wisdom amongst arts organizations that I disagree with and try to fight against? I didn't give a full response during the live interview. Here is a more thoughtful list:

1. *All we need is an endowment.* Of course, if someone drops an endowment in my lap, I will be thrilled to accept it. But the cost of creating an endowment is high since it takes focus away from the key strategic areas for all arts organizations: making great art, marketing aggressively and building the size of the organization's constituency. When revenue is diverted to endowment rather than to making more great art (and marketing it aggressively) the organization can begin to lose its constituents and, therefore, its revenue. And, since every arts organization grows to the point of discomfort anyway — new expenses naturally follow new income — building a larger endowment rarely means financial security. Instead, it almost always translates into a larger budget with the same old tensions.

2. *In our next executive director, we need to hire a strong finance person (often from the for-profit sector) to keep control on expenses.* The problem here is that finance people are experts at measuring problems, not fixing them. Arts organizations need entrepreneurial managers who know how to create income, not intelligent analysts who can tell you how bad things are.

3. *We need to control expenses in order to be healthy.* While some arts organizations do have inflated budgets, far more have inadequate revenue streams. It is far more effective to focus on building new sources of revenue than on saving our way to health.

4. *All artists and arts organizations are spendthrifts.* Wrong. It is amazing how much arts organizations produce with so little. We are not spendthrifts. But we do suffer from a difficulty improving productivity, so our costs rise quickly, and we need to experiment to make great art so there is often

the appearance of waste.

5. *Now is the time to play it safe with programming.* Wrong again. If we all do safe, boring work, we will lose our audiences and our donors. It is the big, surprising projects that build visibility and, therefore, income.

6. *We can attract young audiences by doing more exciting, or higher tech, marketing.* It is not the nature of marketing that attracts any segment of an audience but the work itself. Of course we must use marketing techniques that reach the audience we hope to attract, but simply putting something on Facebook does not guarantee that younger people will come.

7. *Institutional marketing can only be pursued by large, famous organizations.* I have yet to find an arts organization that cannot influence its community by pursuing a campaign that highlights important programming, special events and important announcements. While larger organizations may have a broader range of opportunities to promote themselves, smaller organizations can use their assets to build visibility as well.

I am so glad I was asked this question; it made me recognize how much work is yet to be done.

Why My Peers Are Angry With Me

Many arts managers are angry with me. They do not appreciate my advice *not* to cut programming during this recession. I continue to say that creating large, important projects is central to creating fiscal health. Especially when there is less money for the arts (and there is less money for the arts today), arts organizations must compete harder. As donors decide which organizations to continue to support, the institutions that are doing vital, important work are the ones that will continue to be supported. Not only must the work be interesting, but the marketing of that work and of the institution as a whole must be aggressive and creative.

One arts leader accused me publicly of living in a parallel universe. He was quite upset that his artistic director and his unionized artists threw my advice in his face when he felt he had to make programming cuts. He was dealing with a substantial budget shortfall and saw no other recourse than to cut programming. He was not amused that his artists kept saying, "Michael Kaiser says this, Michael Kaiser says that."

While they were involved in a labor dispute (since resolved), the musicians of the Cleveland Orchestra created a website to state their case. One of the pages was titled, "What Michael Kaiser Would Not Do" and listed all the things I suggest in my writing that the musicians believed were being violated by management. I do not think I want to go back to Cleveland very soon!

I am completely sympathetic with the current plight of my fellow arts managers. It is incredibly scary to go to work not certain if there will be enough money to make payroll. Virtually every arts manager I know is dedicated to the field in which he or she works and wants to produce interesting and important art. They want large audiences. They want big donors. They want a supportive board. And they want their artists to feel cared for and respected.

For the record, I do believe there are times when programming and marketing must be sacrificed, but I believe this should be a last resort, not a first resort. I prefer to cut every other cost imaginable, as my staff will tell you, and to continue to focus on new revenue that is generated from big projects and creative institutional marketing efforts.

There are ways to make programming more vital, even if money is scarce. One is to announce exciting projects for three or four years from now. This makes the organization appear to be thriving, energizes donors and the press and gives the organization years to find the necessary resources to do the project.

Another important tool is to form an artistic joint venture. Joint ventures allow arts organizations to mount larger projects, to consider projects that require skills or talents they do not possess, to extend their marketing and fundraising reach and to design the megaprojects that change the history of the organization.

I am truly sorry that I have caused problems for my peers. My goal has been simply to make their lives easier by suggesting ways to increase revenue. It seems that I have failed.

An Inspiring Trip to New York City

Last week I spent three days in New York City in meetings with the leaders of several arts organizations.

Three of these organizations – The New York City Opera, Dance Theatre of Harlem and the Martha Graham Center of Contemporary Dance – are emerging from periods of great challenge with talented and energizing new leadership. It is gratifying to observe how leaders with vision, ideas and grit can create change in troubled organizations. But it is not surprising. The line between sickness and health in the arts is a slim one. Sick organizations can get healthy relatively quickly because our debts are limited by the small amounts of money people will lend us. (Healthy organizations can get sick rather quickly, because no arts organization has a large enough cushion; arts organizations always grow to the point that they are uncomfortable financially.)

The three other organizations I visited are less well known, if no less important.

The Nuyorican Poets Cafe is a venerable institution that presents groundbreaking works of literature, music, theater, performance art, poetry and visual arts. Nuyorican occupies a unique space in the New York arts ecology. Its young, talented director, Daniel Gallant, is as smart and focused an arts manager as I have met. He is working simultaneously to maintain the quality of the work presented while modernizing the way the cafe operates.

The Lark Play Development Center is a treasure. This organization truly embraces its mission: to facilitate the play creation process for playwrights. Lark allows playwrights to explore their works, to hear them read and to experiment. It creates an environment in which creative people can share ideas, argue and struggle to make art. Hundreds of theater professionals can attest to the impact of this group's work. This is not a flashy organization; one will never read about a gala on the society pages. But its special mission is palpable the minute one walks into its unpretentious space.

Walking into Publicolor is a radically different experience. Publicolor is a unique arts organization that engages at-risk students in their education to prepare them for college and/or careers through a continuum of creative programs that starts with painting their schools. The Publicolor offices are splashed with color; the remarkable staff and board take evident pride in the accomplishments of 'their' students.

At a time when every American arts group is struggling to make ends meet and when the missions of so many arts organizations are being sacrificed, it was a pleasure to spend time with these six arts organizations, each of which is led by people who understand their mission, set clear priorities, implement well and work diligently to find the resources needed.

I would bet my money on all of them.

A Cure for Depression

I have been depressed lately at the lack of spark and creativity I observe from many of our arts organizations. It seems that the leadership — in many cases people like me who have been in the field for 20 years or more — has gotten tired, conservative and frightened. We have become so scared that we won't balance our budgets that we forget that taking risk is a central requisite for arts making. We do not have to succeed every time. But if we never risk, we will never create the important, surprising projects that make people sit up and take notice of our work.

Just as I was feeling very pessimistic, I had a site visit to Dance NYC, a very small but remarkable service organization in New York City. Michelle Burkhart, the head of the organization, has many potent ideas about ways to support the dance community.

One of her most interesting ventures is the Youth Advisory Committee. This is a group of young people, ages 18-30, who are all involved with the world of dance as dancers, administrators, choreographers or presenters. They help the organization mount special projects. For example, the group managed a town hall meeting to discuss ways the younger and older generations of dance lovers and dance professionals could collaborate in the future.

I had a chance to meet with most of the members of the group during my site visit. They are all smart, knowledgeable and dedicated to the dance field. They asked me very smart and penetrating questions about a range of topics: ways presenters could engage more audience members of their generation, arts funding trends in Europe, trends that threaten the dance and larger arts world, etc.

We spent a great deal of time discussing the importance of mentors. I mentioned that I advise all of my arts management fellows at the Kennedy Center to look for jobs where they will have the benefit of a boss who is also a mentor. Like dance itself, which has survived because one generation of dancers/teachers mentors the next, arts management will only build as a field if one generation of managers provides the leadership for the next.

Arts managers tend to work in rather isolated circumstances. Those young managers working in large organizations typically focus on one small segment of the work of that organization without access to many others on staff. Those in very small organizations typically have access to very few people. It is hard under these circumstances to find the support, encouragement and information needed to build a satisfying career.

What Michelle has developed is a method that allows a group of young, smart, ambitious managers to learn from her and from each other. She is a perfect mentor: smart, focused, mature and experienced. And she has the generosity of spirit to make time for 20 20-year-olds who will one day lead our field.

These young mangers are not afraid of new ideas, new concepts and new projects. They take risk daily and seem energized by the possibilities of the future.

I left Dance NYC feeling much more optimistic about the future of dance.

Needed: A Federal Arts Policy

There is frequent discussion about the validity of federal funding for the arts in this nation; most recently, the inclusion of $50 million for employment in the arts in the stimulus package was the source of heated debate.

What we really need is a debate over federal arts *policy*. Most people do not know that no fewer than nine government agencies provide support to arts in this nation. That is not a typo. In addition to the National Endowment for the Arts, the National Endowment for the Humanities and the Institute of Museum and Library Services, arts money is also granted by the Departments of Commerce, Education, State, Agriculture, Defense, and Transportation!

Those of us in the arts are grateful for the many opportunities presented for federal support. The problem is that there is literally no coordination among these agencies on their arts spending, nor is there any central governing philosophy or policy.

For example, grants for arts education are given by several agencies, yet there is no effort to coordinate the educational programming of the arts organizations receiving federal funds. This cannot yield the most effective or efficient results.

There is also no organized process for sharing what has been learned so that every arts organization must learn from its own mistakes. As a result, the federal government has been funding arts education in our public schools for decades, and we still have not implemented a coherent approach to using the arts to benefit our children.

The problem is not that federal funding for the arts is unwarranted; the problem is that we need to be assured, as citizens, that we are getting the most value for our money. What is needed is a coordinated approach to arts grants to ensure that the arts programming supported by federal funds truly serves our national interest.

But how can we accomplish this? How can we coordinate the efforts of so many federal agencies? There has been discussion of the need for a Ministry of Culture in the United States. I am concerned that the formation of such an entity would cost too much and put too little money in the hands of the grassroots arts organizations which truly do the most important arts work in this nation and rarely get the spotlight. (Why do we always use arts celebrities to lobby for government support? Doesn't anyone realize that the American people do not believe their tax dollars should support the work of the most famous and richest performers?)

Instead, we need someone in the administration, perhaps the new chairman of the National Endowment for the Arts, to provide leadership and coordination to ensure that all grants-making agencies are working in a common direction and that the money expended creates an arts ecology that benefits all Americans. We need policies in at least three key areas: sustaining American arts organizations (both large and small), arts education and cultural diplomacy.

The arts have so much to contribute to this nation. We can teach our children to be the creative thinkers that our economy requires now and in the future, we can help rebuild the image of our nation abroad, we can assist in the effort to bolster tourism in the wake of the current economic crisis and we can publicly celebrate the diversity of our nation.

But these vital goals will not be accomplished with the current helter-skelter approach to federal arts funding.

Primal Scream Day

Imagine this scene: Yankee Stadium is filled to the gills with arts managers who wait quietly and expectantly. There are museum directors, opera producers, dance executives, theater managers and symphony administrators. Representatives from marketing, fundraising, finance and production sit side by side with staff from every other area of operations. The scoreboard is ominously dark. Suddenly, it shines with just two words in huge letters: BOARD MEETINGS! The crowd rises as one and screams and screams. Not polite ballpark cheers but bloodcurdling yells. The shouts come from the depth of their souls. The scoreboard eventually goes dark and the crowd begins to quiet once again. Everyone waits with anticipation. Then another three words emerge on the scoreboard: FOUNDATION GRANT PROPOSALS! And the screaming and wailing begins anew.

Welcome to Arts Management Primal Scream Day.

I am sure this is an idea that will reside only in my (addled) mind. But it seems to me that there is a collection of activities arts managers must endure that elicit universal dismay, fear and disgust. Try as we might to manage our organizations in an orderly, professional fashion, there are pitfalls and roadblocks that make all of our jobs more difficult and scary.

Challenges come from rogue board members, uninformed journalists, misguided donors or undisciplined divas. I had one board member ask me to change the music for the children's gala performance of the ballet *Cinderella* scheduled for the next week because she didn't think her children would like the Prokofiev score. I had a donor suggest we fire our orchestra at American Ballet Theatre and simply hire someone to wave his arms in front of the pit; he argued that no one would know that we were dancing to a recording if they could see a fake conductor in action. One important artist refused to appear unless we hired a private jet (at a cost of $56,000) to bring her boyfriend to the Kennedy Center. Early in my career, a foundation funded a program to ensure the fiscal health of a group of arts organizations and then eliminated all funding to the individual organizations!

I know my experiences are far from unique. All arts managers share a common set of problems. Perhaps if we could share our collective unhappiness and scream with abandon, we would be cleansed, refreshed and ready to tackle our difficult jobs anew. Maybe just the act of acknowledging that we all share the same pool of challenges would help us.

Some of you may think the heat has gotten to me. Many of you are probably far more relaxed about the crazy Catch-22s we face, the ill-informed people who affect our work, the problems we encounter when people are really not as dedicated to our missions as we are. Perhaps few of us would be willing to gather for this cathartic experience. But I, for one, would be willing to pay top-ticket to participate in this ritual with my colleagues.

SPECIFIC PROGRAMS AND ART FORMS

Most tenets of arts management work for every art form. In fact, despite major operational differences, most concepts of arts management work for both visual and performing arts (and even for most not-for-profit organizations).

But there are differences between art forms that call for special analysis and attention. Arts education is a crucial area of interest. We in the arts have an opportunity to play a major role as we prepare children to take their places in our new creative economy.

Our orchestras face special problems owing to a difficult economic structure (high fixed costs of musicians), increasing ticket prices and new entertainment options.

And our modern dance ecology is about to experience a major shift as a group of pioneers leave the field to younger, less established dance makers.

Any Given Child

It is a sad reflection on the current state of arts education in our public schools that every arts education program offered by an arts organization sounds good. "We bring children to the symphony." "We offer art classes for children." "We teach dance to at-risk children." Who can argue with any of these programs, especially when the large numbers of children served are mentioned in the next breath? "We serve 11,000 children a year." "We bring the arts to 3,000 students every semester." At the Kennedy Center we boast that we serve 11 million children a year.

But what, if any, good are we doing?

In most cases, the level of arts education enjoyed by a class is solely a function of an individual teacher's passion for the arts. For example, if a third-grade teacher loves the arts, the children are likely to have many arts experiences. When those same children get to fourth grade, they may get no arts education if their teacher does not feel it is important or does not know how to offer it.

Can you imagine your child coming home from fourth grade saying that there would be no math taught that year because the teacher did not like it? But we teach the arts in this episodic manner that cannot foster consistent, quality learning.

And there is a more insidious repercussion of this approach, or non-approach, to arts education. For those at-risk children for whom loss is a central theme — they lose their homes, their parents, their sense of security — we are offering a great gift one year and taking it away the next. The arts bring children into a wonderland that allows them to express themselves and be inspired and carried away. To give a child a chance to dwell in this magical place and then rudely take it away only amplifies this feeling of loss.

Arts education is particularly important at this juncture in our economic history. With manufacturing jobs evaporating, we need more than ever to train our children to be creative, problem-solving members of our economy. The arts allow children to exercise their creativity in ways other subjects cannot.

We must create a smart, affordable approach to arts education. I have been working for the last three years on a new project, Any Given Child, that creates a systematic arts education out of the current hodge-podge approach.

It is called Any Given Child because I want to ensure that any one child gets a solid, meaningful arts education from kindergarten through eighth grade.

This approach utilizes the resources in the schools, the resources of local arts organizations and other agencies, and the resources of the Kennedy Center to create a community-specific approach to arts education.

An audit of the community and the school system reveals what arts education does exist in the school system, what arts organizations and other community groups can offer, and how the school curriculum can help direct an arts education program.

Every arts organization is asked to specialize in a particular grade level and subject matter to meet the needs of the school curriculum. So the symphony might focus on the third grade's study of history and sound, the art museum on the fourth grade's look at other cultures, etc. The Kennedy Center's national arts education programming — including online activities for teachers and students, access to satellite-distributed programming, etc. — are used to fill in voids in available local programming.

The beauty of this approach is that it focuses and coordinates the education efforts of arts organizations while providing a consistent arts education approach. It is also inexpensive. Arts organizations are already providing education services; we do not need to add a great deal of cost to the system to end up with a far more effective approach.

We are hoping to test Any Given Child in several cities over the coming years.

If it works, we will have a new approach to arts education that must benefit every child, and any given child.

Does the Symphonic Orchestra Model Work?

One of the fellows participating in the Kennedy Center Arts Management Institute raised a serious question with me: Can the traditional model of a symphony orchestra work in the United States? He observed that salaries are very high for musicians, conductors and guest artists, and ticket demand is not strong enough to cover most of these costs. High ticket prices are stifling that demand and contributions will continue to have to grow very rapidly to cover inflation.

I cannot argue with this analysis. Somehow the cost structure for American orchestras has risen to the point that every orchestra is likely to struggle to make ends meet.

I do believe that a group of elite orchestras will survive, and even thrive. These orchestras will have the support of their communities, a large thriving fund-raising program and, of course, exciting art.

But the number of orchestras that will be able to achieve this status will be limited. Already we see a series of regional symphonies closing, shortening their seasons or radically restructuring their contracts with musicians. Unfortunately, this is an ugly process that all too often is pursued with a sledgehammer.

Frustrated board members and administrative staff often approach restructuring with a feeling of vengeance: The musicians are getting what they deserve. They are all overpaid anyway argue the leaders of the restructuring.

While supply and demand must be used to evaluate salaries, the salaries for orchestral musicians are virtually always less than the salaries of the stagehands who set up their music stands and chairs! The challenge is that there are so many of them. A major symphony has over 100 musicians; their salaries represent a large and fixed cost.

So boards and administrators who are trying to make ends meet, and do not have the wherewithal to build earned and contributed income, look to reduce this high fixed cost. Musicians, unfortunately, are easy targets, for they have far fewer employment opportunities than the administrators who employ them; when a situation gets ugly the administrator can leave for greener or friendlier pastures; the musicians are left to deal with reduced weeks of work and lower salaries.

In many cases, radical restructuring can be avoided if musicians and administrators embark on a reasonable, long-term planning process that addresses marketing strategies, fundraising approaches and artistic initiatives. In other words, plans for activities that build revenue. But this rarely happens. In fact, the time administrators and musicians communicate most is during union negotiations, when only the cost side of the equation is under consideration.

Without a more enlightened discussion, orchestras are going to continue to fail or to reduce their levels of art and education. I am afraid my Arts Management Institute fellow may be proven right after all.

Why I Worry About Modern Dance

When Merce Cunningham passed away three weeks ago the world lost a dance legend. But I mourn not just the passing of one of the great geniuses of our time but also for the state of modern dance.

Modern dance is one of the glories of American cultural history. From Isadora Duncan to Martha Graham to Alvin Ailey to José Limón and on and on, the ranks of the great modern dancers and choreographers pay tribute to American creativity.

But virtually every great modern dance company was founded more than 40 years ago. Where is the current, not to mention next, generation of great modern dance companies to carry on the torch?

I do not worry as much about ballet companies. While we are still searching for the next Balanchine, ballet companies can continue to produce the great works of the past — from *Giselle* to *Serenade*.

But modern dance depends on new voices, new vocabularies, new works. Since so many modern dance companies are single-choreographer companies, they do not have the ability to sustain themselves easily when their founder passes away. The organization needs an entirely new mission, and that is not so easy to accommodate. (The exception that proves the rule is the Alvin Ailey American Dance Theater. Alvin never intended his company to depend solely on his works. He encouraged many other choreographers to make work for his company; this made the transition to new artistic leadership far easier.)

Merce understood this conundrum. That is why he explicitly planned for the demise of his company in favor of a structure to oversee the dissemination of his works.

But which companies will have the wherewithal — both artistic and financial — to do justice to his masterpieces?

I used to think of Bill T. Jones as the 'young man' of modern dance. But in three short years, Bill T. will be 60 years old!

Where are the young companies that are gathering strength and are prepared to accept the mantle from the Twylas, Pauls, Merces and Marthas?

To be sure, there are wonderfully talented and prolific young modern dance choreographers producing great work. I am fortunate to know, and to present, many of them. But I fear that in our culturally dense world it will be difficult for any of them to attain the level of recognition that their forebears have enjoyed.

And I worry that the level of administrative and board support our young choreographers enjoy is not sufficient to compete with the major musical, ballet and theater institutions.

Does this matter? Does a dance company have to be big and famous to be of importance? I think the answer is no, and yes. A great work of art is a great work of art. It need not be produced in the biggest theaters in world capitals to make a difference.

But I fear that without large role-model organizations representing modern dance around the nation and the world, the field will lose its luster, its ability to attract young dancers and choreographers, and its funding.

I am so lucky to have lived during the golden age of modern dance. I just hope I live long enough to see the next one.

One Approach to Reducing Health Care Costs: The Discipline of Dance

Those of us who work in the arts are convinced of the importance of art for art's sake. We believe that the beauty, inspiration and knowledge one gains from attending performances, exhibitions and workshops have intrinsic value.

But it is undeniable that the arts play other important roles in our society: The arts help to encourage tourism, the arts teach children to be creative thinkers, the arts contribute substantially to the economy, and on and on.

Perhaps because I have spent so much of my career running dance companies, I am particularly interested in the impact of dance education on young people. My work at the Alvin Ailey American Dance Theater (through its remarkable *AileyCamp* program now in 11 cities), American Ballet Theatre (in a program, *Make A Ballet*, we inaugurated at the Frederick Douglass Academy in Harlem), Royal Ballet (in the *Chance to Dance* program offered throughout the greater London area) and in the numerous dance programs sponsored by the Kennedy Center, I have learned that dance is a powerful educational tool for several reasons.

First, one needs no assets besides one's own body. Many children are unable to participate in the arts because their families cannot afford a cello, a piano or art supplies. Yet every child can participate in dance equally; this is the most non-elitist of art forms.

Second, everyone can improve. While not every child can play a violin, every child can and does improve when he or she learns to dance. Not every child becomes a Baryshnikov, but all children can learn to move and express themselves. (Even children with disabilities can benefit from dance training; I have been fortunate to observe children in wheelchairs, children who are blind and children who are deaf dedicated to their dance classes.) As a result, every child who learns to dance can develop the self-respect that is so crucial for future success.

Third, dance teaches discipline. Children who take dance class learn to follow directions, to work as a team while expressing their own individuality and to appreciate the importance of technique and form.

But last, and certainly not least, dance teaches a love of body. Children who dance are far more likely to appreciate their own physical selves. Dance training helps address the obesity problem currently facing our nation. Children who dance regularly are less likely to be overweight; they improve their metabolisms and burn calories. But perhaps most important, children who dance are less likely to participate in the dangerous behaviors that adversely impact the lives of their peers: teen pregnancy, drug abuse, unprotected sex, etc.

It is far cheaper to give a pre-teen dance lessons than it is to treat them for drug abuse, to provide care for the children of children and to treat them for HIV infection.

As we search for ways to reduce health care costs, why not think about providing dance training for every child in this country? It is inexpensive, productive and addresses so many very expensive health care issues.

ECONOMICS AND FINANCE

There is much conventional wisdom about the arts and arts management that is simply wrong. This is not surprising since we are such a young field, and all young areas of study develop theories that are proven wrong over time.

I am particularly concerned about the notion that that "all our organization needs is an endowment." This commonly held belief is not simply wrong, it can be dangerous, placing the focus of the organization on a one-time infusion of capital rather than on developing a healthy art/marketing/fundraising cycle.

The Endowment Conundrum

Ask any 10 board members what would make their organizations more successful and nine of them will say, "All we need is an endowment." An endowment provides 'guaranteed income,' reducing the need for fundraising, and provides a measure of stability for the organization, they argue. Since private fundraising is such a scary concept for so many board members, and feels so uncontrollable, the concept of guaranteed income seems like a godsend.

Of course, I certainly would rather have an endowment than not have one. And if a donor offers me a sizeable contribution to our endowment fund I am, of course, extremely pleased and grateful for the largesse.

But there is a large difference between having an endowment and having fiscal stability, and certainly an immense difference between having an endowment and mounting an endowment campaign.

Endowments do not necessarily create fiscal stability. As we observed in this recession, one cannot depend on endowment earnings. When the capital markets crumble, endowments are worth far less, and the income they generate falls proportionately. Those arts organizations that depend heavily on their endowments certainly suffered over the past two years. Just observe how major universities that have billions of dollars in their endowment funds are struggling at the moment.

But less obviously, I find that organizations with substantial endowments simply raise the level of their budgets to accommodate the investment income generated and don't routinely cut the level of contributed income they plan to raise. If an endowment generates $100,000 of revenue annually, the organization's budget is likely to rise $100,000 a year. In other words, arts organizations always grow to a point where they are uncomfortable. This is not necessarily a bad thing; it means we are more dedicated to pursuing our missions than to creating a period of fiscal relaxation. But it also means that the notion that endowments reduce the need for private fundraising is faulty.

And I would argue that an endowment campaign can actually cause fiscal instability. The cycle that healthy arts organizations enjoy stems from exciting art that is aggressively marketed. This allows the size of the organizational 'family' to grow, yielding larger amounts of revenue. When this revenue is invested in more and better art and marketing, the family continues to grow, revenue continues to rise and everyone is happy.

But when an organization decides to divert its attention and resources to an endowment campaign, this invariably means there is less money, during campaign years, to invest in better programming and marketing. As a result, the family does not grow, revenue does not continue to accelerate and fiscal health is placed in jeopardy. And the amount of endowment that must be raised to make a difference is so large since only 4-6 percent of its principle can be taken as income each year. It takes $3 million of endowment simply to produce $150,000 of annual income. Raising this amount while still raising the annual fund required to continue operations and produce great art is far beyond the fundraising capability of most small and mid-sized organizations.

Some organizations are so disciplined and well-managed that they can balance the needs of programming and marketing with the desire to build the endowment. But these organizations are few and far between.

The next time you hear someone say, "All we need is an endowment," think twice.

The Earned Income Ratio

Arts management is a young field and, like any young field, can take some wrong turns when it comes to theory. Just as it is difficult to argue today that Freud was correct when he wrote that every dream represented some form of wish fulfillment, so arts management has had its share of theories that are difficult to defend.

One favorite early measure of fiscal health used by arts managers was the ratio of earned income (ticket sales, tour fees, auxiliary income, etc.) to total income (earned plus contributed income).

When I started in this field 25 years ago, I was led to believe that the higher the level of earned income to total income the healthier the organization. After all, it was argued, it is far better to earn your own way than to rely on contributions from corporations, foundations and individuals.

I learned the fallacy of this argument when I arrived at the Alvin Ailey American Dance Theater. The group was proud that it earned 75 percent of its income; the Board members believed that it showed self-reliance and tremendous demand. To me this was not a strength. It simply meant that this was an organization that didn't know how to raise money! And worse, it was forcing the dancers to perform more often than was healthy in order to earn tour fees that paid the bills.

Other organizations that serve very poor communities, conversely, have very low levels of earned income. Their missions demand that they produce art for very low ticket prices if they are going to make their art accessible to people with little or no discretionary income. They must rely on contributed income for a large share of their total revenue. This is not bad; it is an essential part of the strategy for these groups.

The level of earned income as a percent of revenue differs from organization to organization. There is not a better ratio, nor a worse one. There are simply implications of having strong or weak levels of earned income.

Arts organizations with strong earned income must protect it by developing important art and by ensuring their programmatic marketing efforts are significant. If the environment is changing and it seems unlikely that these steps will be enough to protect the level of earned income, these organizations must develop stronger fundraising capabilities.

Organizations with low levels of earned income must develop the strong institutional marketing programs required to ensure growth of contributed income. If it will be difficult to continue to build the level of contributed revenue, they must also explore ways to bolster earned income through additional ticket sales or touring activity or by finding new auxiliary sources of earned income (rentals, merchandising, parking fees, food service, etc.).

But when organizations work to change the earned income ratio and explicitly change strategies, they must ensure that they are not coincidentally — and unintentionally — also changing missions. The arts group that services people with low income levels and tries to raise its earned income level by raising prices may be disenfranchising the very people it wishes to serve.

PEOPLE

Writing a weekly column gives me the opportunity to pay tribute to my arts heroes. In many cases, these are people whose names are unfamiliar to the majority of my readers. For as much as I respect and even worship great dancers, singers, violinists, actors, etc., I am more fascinated by the people behind the scenes.

I encourage the world to celebrate the accomplishments of these arts executives. Not simply for their benefit but for the benefit of the arts in general. We need more and better arts managers. We need to spend more time and money training arts managers. We need better tools to differentiate the strong leader from those not capable of running an arts institution. And we need to celebrate those who are successful in the hopes that others of talent will be attracted to the field.

Remembering Denise Jefferson

The dance world lost a giant on July 17 when Denise Jefferson passed away. I would venture to say that hundreds of thousands of dance lovers, who may not even know her name, have great reason to celebrate her memory.

Denise, the director of the Ailey school, was one of the four pillars of the Ailey organization for decades. Along with Judith Jamison, Sylvia Waters and Masazumi Chaya, Denise provided a rock-solid foundation for the organization. It is not surprising that over 85 percent of the dancers who currently perform with the Alvin Ailey American Dance Theater received training at the school. And many more of her students went on to important careers with other major dance companies.

Denise invested herself in every child in the school. She knew that by teaching children to dance, she was also teaching them to respect their bodies. This was a great gift for the young people in the school. She knew there were life lessons to be learned through dance that could benefit every child, not just the most talented who would eventually become professional dancers.

She was kind and caring, but she was also tough. She knew that the benefits of dance required discipline, hard work and an endless striving for perfection. She would not compromise on quality and she would not tolerate dancers who did not work to their full potential.

But anyone who worked hard received her admiration and her support. Forever. Denise cared about her students long after they left her school.

Denise became a special friend of mine when I became executive director of the Ailey organization in 1991. She taught me a great deal about the various techniques that an Ailey dancer had to learn and about the history of African-American choreography.

We discussed ways to make the school more visible and better able to meet the needs of a very diverse student body.

But Denise was also my special personal tutor in all things African-American. She was an unembarrassed guide into the world of black customs and culture. I will always love her for the day she showed up at work, covered from head to toe in clothing. She quickly raised and lowered a sleeve to fulfill my request, rude as it was, to see what 'ash' was. I must admit the glimpse was so fast I didn't see what all the fuss was about!

Denise and I did not agree on everything. Her three-hour recitals in our non-air-conditioned studios in June seemed far too long to me. She disagreed. Every child who had worked so hard all year should have a chance to dance, she said. We argued about this for three years. Even after I left the Ailey organization Denise and I would argue about the length of recitals.

I will miss arguing with her.

And I will miss my special guide. I will miss her honesty and humor and grace and beauty.

The Transition at Alvin Ailey

The Alvin Ailey organization has recently announced that Robert Battle will replace Judith Jamison as artistic director next year. Robert will have one year to work with Judith to prepare for this huge assignment. There was much to dissect in this surprising announcement. Mr. Battle is very young, he has run a very small dance company and will take over the largest modern dance organization in the world, he never danced with the Ailey company, etc.

I ran the Ailey organization from 1991-1993 as executive director and came to appreciate the tremendous strengths of Judith Jamison. She was relatively new as artistic director at that time, but she was very clear on her artistic goals for the institution. She wanted to preserve the best of Alvin's choreography while bringing new dance makers to the organization. Of course, she had the benefit of years of counsel from Alvin Ailey himself; in fact, Judith always talks about "standing on Alvin's shoulders." She has been a remarkable steward for the organization, and taking her place will be a formidable challenge.

For the past 15 years, Judith has had a remarkable partner in Sharon Gersten Luckman as executive director. I hired Sharon to be my development director at Ailey. It was the best hire I ever made in my career. Sharon and Judith have created an astonishing juggernaut that has allowed the Ailey organization to thrive. The new fantastic building, the expansion of the Ailey school, the increased touring, the larger presence in New York City — all have come from the remarkable partnership of Judith and Sharon. The way this transition has proceeded is just another in a long line of successes.

For me, in fact, the amazing aspect of this announcement was how smooth the selection process seemed from the outside.

The institution of Ailey has now had to replace artistic directors twice in the past 20 years. These transitions were handled with astonishing professionalism and focus. There was none of the drama that has accompanied such transitions at other organizations. The board, artistic leadership and administrative staff all seem united and genuinely happy.

This latest transition is perhaps the more remarkable. Twenty years ago, Alvin asked Judith to take over for him on his death bed. There was no question that a new leader had to be found and Judith was a natural heir to the position.

But this transition did not have to happen. Judith is still an amazing, potent woman. She could have continued to occupy this important position. It was her decision that it was time to step down. It was her decision to participate fully in this search process. It was her discipline and her deep love for the Ailey company that made the search process move gracefully over the past year.

I can't imagine a better exclamation point to her remarkable career than the way she has facilitated this beautiful transition. Her legacy will astonish and educate anyone who studies it for centuries to come.

Verdery Roosevelt's Departure

The dance world was surprised recently to learn that Verdery Roosevelt was leaving her job as executive director of Ballet Hispanico. When most executive directors leave their jobs it barely causes a ripple. We are more interested in who will become the new executive than we are in the person who just left.

But Verdery is an institution. She has been at the helm of Ballet Hispanico for 31 years. She is largely responsible for building a thriving, important dance organization, one of the most important Latino arts organizations in the nation. For an organization that thrives on the dramatic, Verdery was always cool and collected.

It is unusual these days for an executive to last even 10 years with one organization; to last more than three decades is an astonishing accomplishment.

It is not that she didn't have other options. Verdery has been asked on numerous occasions if she wanted to leave Ballet Hispanico and run larger, 'more prestigious' organizations.

But she always said no thank you.

Verdery truly and passionately supported the mission of her organization and the dreams of her artistic partner, Tina Ramirez, who retired last year. Characteristically, Verdery stayed on to ensure a smooth transition at the organization she loved.

At a time when so many people question the motives of arts executives, when it is assumed that we all care more for the bottom line than for the artistic mission of our organizations, Verdery is the shining example that such generalizations are untrue and dangerous. This is not to say she was not a great steward of the fiscal health of Ballet Hispanico; but she knew that good art creates good financial health, and she was truly and properly supportive of her artists.

In fact, watching her work was an object lesson in good arts management: She taught me more about staying true to one's artists while doing what was best for the organization than anyone.

And she did it in her understated way: always professional, always kind, always supportive, yet with a directness that suggested she would never work any way but the way she felt was best for her organization. Not surprisingly, donors adored her, especially professional donors such as corporations and foundations. They always knew that when they made a grant to Verdery, the money would be spent wisely, the project would proceed in a smart, planned way and the arts world would benefit.

The dance world will be poorer without her at the helm of Ballet Hispanico. There is not a large pool of people like Verdery, with the sophisticated knowledge matched by intense passion, ready to run arts organizations. Unfortunately, we have not done a good job of creating the next generation of arts leaders.

I do not know her plans for the future. Perhaps she does not know herself.

But I hope for all of our sakes she doesn't stop leading by her shining example.

The Remarkable Barney Simon

People across the nation have been asking me why I have embarked on my 50-state "Arts in Crisis" speaking tour. I always answer, truthfully, that I am concerned that so many arts organizations are making poor decisions as they attempt to cope with the current economic crisis. They are cutting programming first, rather than last, and sacrificing long-term revenue for short-term expense savings.

But there is a second, equally truthful, motivation for this tour and for all of my national and international efforts to educate arts managers: Barney Simon.

Barney Simon was the founder and artistic director of the Market Theatre in Johannesburg, South Africa. He made the Market a place where white artists and black artists could work together. In a South Africa brutalized by apartheid, this was not simply a noble mission, it was an act of courage. Barney trained a generation of South African artists; virtually anyone working in South African theater today was influenced by Barney or one of his disciples.

For several decades, Barney produced and directed many of the most important works of indigenous South African theater. He was the first to direct the works of his good friend, Athol Fugard. He exported these plays across Europe and the United States. These works educated us about the horrors of apartheid and moved us to act.

It is not an overstatement to say that Barney Simon played a major role in the ending of apartheid.

I met Barney, ironically, just after the end of apartheid when Nelson Mandela was elected president of South Africa.

I worked with Barney to save his Market Theatre, which, of course, had never received a government subsidy during the era of apartheid and was entirely reliant on private donations, an oddity in South Africa. With the end of apartheid, most gifts that were required of foreign corporations doing business in South Africa were cancelled, putting the Market at risk.

While I was Barney's consultant, he taught me far more than I taught him. He taught me that I had a responsibility to use the arts for the good of people, not for self-aggrandizement. He taught me that the arts are a powerful weapon of change and that we have an obligation to use this weapon wisely. He taught me that I had to widen my perspective on arts and take more artistic risk.

This is why I have devoted much of my life over the past 10 years to teaching, to international exchange and now to working with arts group struggling in this current economic environment. I do not have Barney's artistic talents, but he exhorted me to find a way to use what I know to help others.

Barney died, far too young, in 1995. But his spirit lives on and challenges me every day.

My Arts Management Hero: Babs Mollere

It was a joy to go back to New Orleans on my "Arts in Crisis" tour and to meet the many dedicated arts professionals who work there. I have been a steady visitor to this beautiful city since a few months after Hurricane Katrina. We at the Kennedy Center adopted the Louisiana Philharmonic Orchestra immediately after the hurricane and devoted our efforts to saving this wonderful arts organization.

Over the past four and a half years, I have developed my New Orleans family of arts managers and musicians and board members. The progress the symphony has made since those first parlous days is amazing.

I credit this success to a patient, mature group of musicians who truly feel ownership of the orchestra and to a trio of complementary leaders: the dedicated chairman, Hugh Long, the energetic young maestro, Carlos Miguel Prieto, and, especially, its executive director, Babs Mollere.

Babs is one of the most amazing arts managers I have ever encountered on all my travels across the nation and the globe.

We met at a difficult time but in a humorous way. Immediately after Katrina, we decided to offer our turnaround assistance to a struggling arts organization affected by the hurricane. The LPO seemed a logical candidate since its theater had been destroyed and its subscribers and donors were scattered across the nation, as were its musicians, staff and board. I traced Babs to her temporary office in Baton Rouge, called her and offered my help. Her response was a succinct: "I don't know who you are."

Since then, we have gotten to know each other very well. I have watched Babs handle extraordinary challenges that most arts managers never experience. After Katrina, there was nothing: no housing, no theater, no audience, no subscription series, no donors. Nothing. Walking in downtown New Orleans after the hurricane was like entering a city where a neutron bomb had been detonated. There were no people. When checking into a hotel, one was given a towel, a bottle of water and a warning that there was virtually no staff on the premises.

From this emptiness, Babs has systematically built a performance season in a variety of venues, created a staff, developed a donor base and recreated a subscriber base, virtually from scratch. She has done it with humor, hard work and a vision for what the LPO can and should be.

The orchestra has given a series of major performances (Yo-Yo Ma was a guest soloist this season), created an education program that now reaches every parish in the state of Louisiana, established a regional touring program most orchestras would envy and commissioned new works that speak to the diverse community the LPO serves. In particular, the LPO has celebrated the jazz heritage of its city in numerous collaborations.

And, by the way, the LPO has not had a deficit the past several seasons, a testimony to Babs, the board, the musicians and the community they all serve.

It is a joy to observe, to support and to engage with these amazing people.

The End of Morphoses

When Christopher Wheeldon announced he was leaving Morphoses, the company he founded three years ago, it reminded me just how hard it is to start an arts organization.

Chris had everything going for him when he began his company; he is remarkably successful and famous, deeply loved by many in the dance world and admired by even more. He claimed headlines in the *New York Times* when he announced his organization and received reviews from serious critics for every performance.

Numerous presenters, including we at the Kennedy Center, lined up to present Morphoses. We had planned for Chris and his dancers to be part of our *Ballet Across America* series this Spring and to have a week of their own next season.

Everyone, including Chris, knew that creating a dance company was more than simply creating dances. Building an administrative infrastructure and a board, establishing a fundraising base and creating an audience would all be challenges. But no new dance company in my memory was better positioned. Through his work at New York City Ballet and American Ballet Theatre, alone, he had numerous contacts in the funding world.

But after just three years, he has left. The company has not folded; it has over $1 million in the bank. But the board and staff remaining must now consider what to do without its founding artistic motivation.

The toll of constant fundraising, board-building and marketing, the time taken from choreographing and, finally, working without a corps of steady dancers became too much for Chris.

Why should he spend time wooing a board when he can make dances for the greatest dance companies in the world? Why should he work with an ever-changing group of dancers when he can make ballets on established corps in

London, New York and San Francisco?

It is hard not to sympathize.

But it is also important to use this moment to commemorate the remarkable persistence and hard work of those who did stick with their companies for decades and decades. Those whose initial work was not covered by the *New York Times*. Those who had to scrounge for the most meager budgets and who were not offered many performance opportunities.

I am thinking of people like Joan Myers Brown, Trisha Brown, Jeraldyn Blunden, José Limón, Elisa Monte, Paul Taylor, Alvin Ailey, Merce Cunningham, George Faison and so many others.

These pioneers created dance organizations that have contributed to the dance community and to the national arts ecology for decades. Our dance heritage would not be the rich cultural jewel it is without their struggles.

They stood by their dancers and by their organizations in the very difficult early years. They did not have people asking to serve on boards, they did not have presenters competing to engage them, they did not even get reviewed.

They created magic with so very little.

They are true arts heroes.

ARTS IN CRISIS TOUR

I was fortunate to be able to travel to every state of the union (plus Puerto Rico and the District of Columbia) in a 14- month period ending in July 2010. The purpose of my trip was to discuss in public forums the ways arts organizations should deal with the recession.

In total, 11,000 arts managers, artists and board members came to my sessions in 69 cities from Anchorage to Miami.

Each session was moderated by one or several local arts executives. But despite this local flavor, the sessions were remarkably similar; the questions centered on issues of board management, fundraising, artistic planning and marketing.

I know I learned as much as I taught — there is a wealth of knowledge and experience in every city in this nation, as well as a determination that the arts must continue to play a vital role.

Where Are the Arts Important?

As I was preparing for my "Arts in Crisis" tour stops in a series of southern states, I was reflecting on the claims of too many politicians that the arts are the province of the elite in big coastal cities like New York and Los Angeles. This is used as an excuse for denigrating public support for the arts and, by extension, the arts themselves. The argument goes that investing in the arts only affects a very small, very rich and very concentrated segment of our population.

While it is true that many of our largest arts organizations are in large northeastern cities and that these arts groups have raised their ticket prices so high as to make them unaffordable for many, the arts play a vital role in virtually every community across the nation. It is not simply rich New Yorkers who care about music or dance or theater. People of all backgrounds and income levels are involved with the arts across the United States.

Why else would 400 enthusiastic people come to my presentation in Kalamazoo, Michigan, and 750 attend in Kansas City, Missouri? In fact, I have already spoken with over 7,000 people on the 38 tour stops to date. I have met with passionate advocates for arts and arts education in Tulsa, Des Moines and Wichita. These arts leaders were no different in knowledge, sophistication or creativity than their counterparts in New York, Chicago or San Francisco.

This thought struck home as I was preparing for my recent appearance in Meridian, Mississippi. I started thinking about examples of great art and artists from the region.

I remembered that my favorite singer of all time, Leontyne Price, came from Laurel, Mississippi, less than an hour away from Meridian. What an immense loss to the world if Miss Price had not been allowed to experience the joy of singing as she grew up in Laurel. And my life would have been different if she had not given a recital in the Loew's movie theater in New Rochelle, New York, when I was 16. Hearing her sing and meeting her after the concert changed my life.

And I remembered that Ethan Stiefel, one of the world's great ballet dancers, came from northern Wisconsin where his father was a prison warden. I know American ballet would be poorer if he had not been allowed to study dance. Ethan was a brilliant principal dancer at New York City Ballet and American Ballet Theatre and is now the dean of the School of Dance at the North Carolina School of the Arts. Twyla Tharp came from Portland, Indiana, and Terrence McNally was raised in Corpus Christi, Texas. The list goes on and on.

The arts affect every region of this nation. I am learning this on my tour. We ignore the power and potency of the arts if we assume that the only important work is happening in the big northeast or west coast cities. Without the availability of art and arts education throughout the country during the past centuries, our cultural heritage, a glory of our nation, would have been vastly diminished. Why is today any different?

My Visit to Kalamazoo

Two months ago I decided to embark on a 50-state "Arts in Crisis" tour. The purpose of this tour was to talk about the issues facing arts organizations in the current economic environment and to discuss ways to address these challenges. As I planned the tour, I thought I would visit the biggest city in every state. I believed, erroneously, that this would give me exposure to the most arts organizations and managers. Then I received a letter from Jim McIntyre, a board member of the Arts Council of Greater Kalamazoo, asking me to visit his city. Like other cities in Michigan, Kalamazoo has been hard-hit by the recession, and many arts organizations there are struggling. Jim had another compelling reason for asking me to visit Kalamazoo. His children had attended my sister's school, Bread and Roses, decades ago, and he remained a close friend of my sister Susan.

Kalamazoo is a relatively small city. There are just over 75,000 people who live in the city and approximately 250,000 people who live in the entire county.

And yet my "Arts in Crisis" session in Kalamazoo drew over 400 people! The ballroom of the Radisson Hotel was filled to capacity. The mayor of the city was there, as was the former mayor who is now a state representative. (A group of community leaders — business people, a college president, foundation executives and educators — had a breakfast with me before the session to educate me about the nature of the arts community and its issues.) The issues raised by the audience were no different than those raised in New York, Cleveland, San Diego or Baltimore, all substantially larger cities. The arts managers, board members and artists who came to the session were all facing budget cuts, reduced state funding, a rapidly changing and diminishing corporate community and low morale.

They asked pertinent, detailed and intelligent questions about ways to maintain their theater companies, ballet companies, symphonies and education programs. The mayor asked about best practices in arts education. He believes that the arts are a necessary part of the education of every child in his city but was concerned about ways to pay for it.

Board members asked about how boards should change as organizations mature. Artists asked how they could help their organizations cope with the current crisis. And the arts administrators asked how they could reduce budgets without irreparably harming their organizations.

In general, there was great concern that the fabric of the arts in Kalamazoo not be destroyed by the current crisis.

But the overwhelming feeling from every person in the room was that the arts were not dispensable in this environment. The feeling from top to bottom was that the arts are central to the healthy ecology of the city.

It was a truly inspirational meeting. Here, in the middle of America, in a small city, in the state most battered by the recession, was an entire community saying that the arts matter, that the health of their community depended in great measure on the health of their arts programming. They were determined to work together — the arts community, the business community, the political community and the educational community — to maintain the vitality of the arts in their city.

Next time government officials in Washington or elsewhere say that the arts are elitist, that they only serve the largest cities, that all arts funding finds its way to the coasts, or that everyday people don't care about the arts, I am going to suggest they visit Kalamazoo, Michigan. I think they will learn a great deal, as I did.

My Visit to Kansas City

One of the stops on my "Arts in Crisis" tour that I looked forward to most was the visit to Kansas City, Missouri. Twenty-four years ago I started my arts management career in Kansas City, running the Kansas City Ballet. Going back to the Lyric Theatre, where the ballet gave many memorable performances, was a true homecoming.

The visit did not disappoint. Approximately 750 people showed up for my session, far more than in any other city. The session began with the entire Kansas City Symphony performing the Academic Festival Overture by Brahms. This was the first time a musical ensemble performed before my session and it set the perfect tone. (This piece is special to me since it was written for the German town of Breslau, now part of Poland, where my father was born and raised.) Michael Stern, the dynamic music director of the symphony conducted the orchestra and my interview.

Sitting on the stage of the Lyric Theatre, I could not help but remember the first years of my career, both the successes and the failures. The very first performances during my tenure were a disaster. I had wasted the entire marketing budget on a clever idea that we could not implement well. We sold fewer tickets to those performances than to any other in the history of the company. It was not an auspicious debut, but it taught me so much about the scale required for a strong marketing effort.

For our next set of performances, we built a relationship with the Girl Scouts who purchased thousands of tickets; these sales resulted in the first sell-out performances in our history. Some of my board members, who were used to buying tickets minutes before a performance, were both thrilled and annoyed that they simply could not buy a ticket to the final performance!

And by the end of that season, we had a new relationship with Alvin Ailey that allowed us to perform many of his works to great acclaim. The artistic growth of the company was due entirely to the good taste of Todd Bolender, our artistic director. His vision, complemented by a strong institutional marketing drive, allowed the company to thrive.

The Kansas City Ballet is a classic example of an art-focused turnaround. Without Todd's strong repertory choices, his able support team of ballet mistress Una Kai and school director Diana Adams, and the guest artists he attracted to set ballets and teach (John Taras, Violette Verdy and Melissa Hayden my first year alone), the company could not have attracted the press attention nor negotiated a debut tour to New York City that were so central to our success.

The substantial community of arts sponsors came to think of the company differently. I joke that the tag line for the company when I arrived was "the ballet company that can't make payroll." And it was true. Every two weeks we called around town to see who could contribute something so we could pay the dancers their meager wages. After the artistic and marketing successes of our first season, the community came to think of the Kansas City Ballet as the 'hot organization' in the city. Not surprisingly, we were able to increase our fundraising and ticket revenue substantially and pay off our entire accumulated deficit in one season.

What is important about this story is that the staff of the Kansas City Ballet was very small — only four full-time people on the administrative team. It does not take a large organization to develop important art nor to create a stronger marketing profile.

The lessons I learned in Kansas City paved the way for the remainder of my career. Sitting on the Lyric Theatre stage, surrounded by so many friends and colleagues, board members and donors, I felt a tremendous surge of gratitude.

Visiting Grand Rapids

At first blush, my "Arts in Crisis" tour stop in Grand Rapids seemed ill-timed.

After all, I am touring all 50 states to discuss approaches for dealing with the current economic crisis; to discuss the mistakes arts organizations make when they reduce programming or play it safe in this environment.

Yet I arrived the first week of ArtPrize, an innovative new arts project that has electrified the city and the region.

For those few who have not heard of ArtPrize, any artist was invited to create a work of art and show it at indoor and outdoor venues across downtown Grand Rapids. Ultimately, 1,262 artists installed works — from simple drawings to huge, elaborate sculptures. I was particularly taken with a series of portraits, silk-screened on perfectly formed mounds of salt. The public was invited to see the works and to vote on their favorites. More than 334,000 votes were cast and the winner received prize money of $250,000, an extraordinary sum.

To say that the region was consumed by ArtPrize is an understatement. Every person I met asked if I had seen many works, which were my favorites and whether I was voting. Venues were packed at noon on a Wednesday. Buses filled with school children were touring the city. Thousands of people turned out for a performance art event: 100,000 paper airplanes flown from the roof of a building. To those of us who believe that art has the power to inspire and enliven our communities, this was a glorious example.

ArtPrize is the brainchild of Rick DeVos. (For complete disclosure, Rick's mother Betsy is a trustee of the Kennedy Center.) Rick has created an innovative, successful, energizing arts project that was conceived of and staged during this great economic crisis. And not in New York or Los Angeles or Chicago, but in Grand Rapids, Michigan, a state that has felt this recession as much as any and where the state government slashed the budget of the state arts council by 71 percent the day before I arrived.

ArtPrize is the perfect example of what I discuss on my tour: Arts organizations that do great work and market it well can thrive at any time — even during a major recession in a depressed state. There is a tremendous hunger for innovation and inspiration at this time. How else to explain the thousands of creative submissions, the hundreds of thousands of people registering to vote and the many, many more who simply came to observe?

The mistake arts organizations make is to pull in their horns, limit creativity, reduce important programming and play it safe. The public sees through this approach; they do not have money to waste on boring programming.

And arts organizations that become less interesting to their audiences also become less interesting to their donors. It is simple to blame 'the economy' for a lack of ticket sales or contributions, but it invariably results in larger measure from a lack of quality programming and marketing.

The people running ArtPrize talk happily about prospects for the future and working to cope with increased demand in future years. Who would have guessed that the perfect lesson for coping successfully with a failing economy would come from Grand Rapids?

My Trip to San Juan

I recently went to San Juan, city number 40 on the Kennedy Center's "Arts in Crisis" tour. I knew that I would have to alter my message a bit since Puerto Rico's arts organizations do not enjoy the same level of private philanthropy as do those in the 50 states.

There is a European flavor to the funding of the arts in Puerto Rico; government is a key sponsor of a few select organizations, corporations are the most prominent source of private funding and there is but one major foundation that supports the arts. Individual donors are few and far between. Even board members act more like overseers; they are not routinely expected to make financial contributions or to play a central role in fundraising. Arts organizations that do not receive government funding have to rely on earned income and on any bit of support they can develop from the small group of private funders.

The recession, not surprisingly, has had a major impact on virtually all arts endeavors. So, like everywhere else, there is fear. Artists are scared, as are managers and board members.

But these remarkably open people were very accepting of my message. They understood that reducing programming was not a healthy way to proceed. They agreed that they under-market their artistic programming and that they were unlikely to build a larger philanthropic base until the community better appreciates their work. And, of key importance, they accepted that their boards would have to change dramatically and quickly. Even the numerous board members who attended my session seemed to appreciate that they, like their cousins serving on European boards, needed to revise their job descriptions.

As the pressure to increase private funding dramatically is felt here in Puerto Rico, as it is being felt in Europe and South America and Asia, boards will have to change their roles.

Therefore, this is a scary time of transition. Board members, who currently are wonderful ambassadors for their organizations and who take their obligation to evaluate and approve plans and budgets seriously, will have to play a far larger role in fundraising. And charity must begin at home; board members will have to become substantial donors to their own organizations.

I have every confidence that this will happen in those organizations that learn how to make it fun to be an individual donor, approach individual fundraising with discipline and creativity and are willing to restructure their boards.

The arts in Puerto Rico must survive; there is a tremendous love for creativity and music and dancing and the visual arts. All those present at my session were deeply proud of the work of their organizations and eager for me to come to their performance, school or exhibition. So many important artists of all genres emerge from these groups. And the enthusiastic reception I received was evidence that the arts community appreciates the need for change.

But the leaders of this community must work diligently to create a new funding model and a new approach to governance to assure the vitality of the arts ecology.

What I Am Learning on My Tour

My 50-state, 69-city tour is almost over; I will make my last presentation on July 16 in Boise, Idaho.

The tour has been both inspiring and depressing at the same time.

It is inspiring to see so many communities that value the arts and so many individuals determined to maintain arts in their cities and states. I estimate that some 11,000 people will have attended an "Arts in Crisis" tour presentation. Each of these individuals cares deeply for the arts in their hometowns.

When I visited Billings, Montana, some people drove as much as six hours each way to make sure they could take part in the discussion. Numerous South Dakotans drove for hours to Pierre for our session there. Many politicians came to these sessions as well — mayors, city councilmen, school superintendants, state senators, congressmen — displaying their concern and interest in the role the arts play in their communities.

In too many cities to name, new or restored theaters and museums provided spectacular venues for our presentations and for the arts. Clearly there was enough interest in these cities to invest millions of dollars to ensure a proper home for the arts.

And in virtually every city, the press was present at these events. Newspaper, television and radio journalists have given this tour an astonishing level of coverage.

One had to come away from this tour with an overwhelming feeling of optimism for the future of the arts in America.

But I was depressed to see how many venues I visited presented performances that were entirely interchangeable with performances at other venues.

It is not that the art was bad. It simply was not special or unique to the organization. In other words, there was simply no evidence of curation. Kevin McKenzie, the artistic director of American Ballet Theatre, was the first person to teach me about how one must curate a season, selecting works that fit together and making sure the audience was learning along the way. I have extrapolated from his concept and believe that curating a special project or festival is an important part of being a good presenter.

Of course it is wonderful for any community to experience the Alvin Ailey American Dance Theater or a recital by Yo-Yo Ma. But shouldn't each venue also be creating projects unique to its community?

Presenters must do more than fill slots. They must develop projects that will build excitement and reputation for creativity and excellence. These projects can be interesting amalgams of guest artists or organizations or work that is produced specially by the presenting organization.

Why can't a mid-sized presenter create a festival, perhaps in collaboration with a local producing organization, museum or educational institutions?

When I talk about the need for large, transformational projects, heads always nod up and down in my "Arts in Crisis" sessions and people tell me how inspiring this concept is. But as I look at the schedules for U.S. presenters, with few exceptions, the programming has not changed.

Perhaps I must give it more time. Perhaps in three or four years we will see great new projects that have taken that long to gestate.

But I am afraid my tour will not have accomplished enough to justify the expense of time and money if the programming in our theaters does not change dramatically.

My 50-State Tour

I just completed a 50-state, 69-city tour across the entire United States. I traveled 83,000 miles and spoke with nearly 11,000 artists, arts managers, board members, elected officials and concerned citizens.

We discussed both generic approaches for dealing with (and not dealing with) an economic downturn, as well as local arts issues and concerns.

The motivation for this tour came from my fear that the recession would set many arts organizations on a path that would create problems for years to come. When an arts organization's first response to a fiscal crisis is to cut programming and marketing, bad things are sure to happen.

Surprisingly, and thankfully, the name of the tour, "Arts in Crisis," surprised people in many communities. Many people said they were happy to come and talk about how to improve their organizations, but they didn't feel in crisis. Yes, things were tougher than they had been, but they did not feel their organizations were in danger.

When I started the tour, I thought I might write a book about the experience. I thought it could be interesting to illuminate the differences in the arts ecologies between each community.

I was wrong. While there is certainly great variability in the intensity with which the recession has influenced each city, the issues faced by arts organizations are remarkably consistent.

How do you make a board more productive? How can we take advantage of new technologies to sell more tickets? How do we raise more money? What should start-up arts organizations focus on? Where do we find trained staff or volunteers? These questions, or variations on these questions, were asked on every stop of the tour.

There will be no book after all; it would be too dull. I could write about the legroom challenges of regional airplanes, the best places to eat in Meridian,

Mississippi, or Billings, Montana, or the remarkable physical beauty of our country, but I would have nothing to add to the others who write about travel.

But this does not mean I did not learn anything of value on my tour. I learned of the vibrancy of the arts in America. I learned that arts leaders simply will not give up. I learned that some of the most interesting artists and most entrepreneurial arts managers are working in some of our smallest cities. And I learned that we need to give these managers and their boards a far better education if we want the arts to flourish.

Some have said I did this tour to promote myself. If so, I am incredibly inefficient and deserve to be fired. (I reach more people with one post on this blog than all the visits combined.) Indeed, we planned several stops in less-populous areas where expectations for attendance were low. Regardless of size, participants in every city shared common concerns and displayed a passion for the arts that inspired me tremendously.

And if the Kennedy Center is doing a better job of fulfilling its mandate to be the national cultural center, then I certainly don't mind the attendant publicity. It is my job to create visibility for my organization.

But the overwhelming feeling I have is gratitude for the people who came to the sessions (often driving four or more hours to do so), the 69 local moderators who interviewed me and the hundreds of people who helped organize the events. I know I was given a most rare opportunity and I am truly grateful.

EPILOGUE

We live in a time of great transition. Our economy is changing, our social mores are evolving (not always for the better) and the way we communicate and spend our leisure time is transforming every year.

It is not a simple time to run any enterprise, including an arts organization. How we, as an industry, adapt to the changes in our nation and our world will determine whether we remain a part of the lives of those in our communities.

It is difficult not to be fearful of the future.

But the solutions will not come from those of my generation. There is a large, passionate cadre of young people who are far better positioned to see the arts through the new century.

I remain both hopeful and grateful.

What I Am Giving Thanks for This Year (2009)

The current economic downturn has indeed created a crisis for virtually every sector of the economy, especially those of us in the not-for-profit arena. Yet during this Thanksgiving week, I believe we in the arts have a great deal to be thankful for even in this troubled time.

First, we must be grateful that our arts organizations have proven to be so resilient. At the beginning of this year, there were predictions that as many as 10,000 American not-for-profit arts organizations would go bankrupt as a result of this recession. In truth, nowhere near that number will go out of business. Arts organizations suffer and bend, but we rarely break. We mourn those organizations that have disbanded; they are a great loss to their communities and to the nation's arts ecology. But we celebrate the thousands more that are still producing important work.

As a corollary, I am also grateful to the more than 120 arts management professionals who have volunteered to be mentors in the Kennedy Center's "Arts in Crisis" initiative since February of this year. These dedicated executives from across the nation have given their time and expertise, and frequently their own personal resources, to ensure that as many arts organizations as possible survive this difficult time. The consulting support they are providing to other arts organizations has proven to be invaluable.

We must also be grateful to those donors who have continued to be generous despite the recession. Foundations that have temporarily increased their spending rates to avoid making drastic cuts to their grantees have been true heroes. When so many other donors have had to cut their grants, those foundations who have increased their spending rates have taken up the slack.

So have the hundreds of thousands of individuals who have maintained their giving in this precarious environment. Gifts from individual donors have always been less cyclical than those from institutional donors; arts organizations ignore the creation of a solid individual donor program at their own risk. And a big thank-you to the U.S. Congress for voting $50 million in stimulus funds for the arts and an additional $25 million for the

NEA and the NEH. At a time when most state and local agencies are cutting arts grants, these increases are of immense importance to the arts world.

Many of our individual donors are also our board members. As so many boards are stressed and stretched, we must acknowledge that our board members are volunteers with no obligation to serve. Yet so many of our arts organizations could not survive without the involvement of our board members. Wherever I travel across the globe, I am always asked why our board members are so generous of time, spirit and resources. This is a uniquely American phenomenon and one which we must not take for granted.

Finally, I am grateful that in good times or bad, artists continue to create such remarkable work. I have seen the most wonderful performances and exhibitions this year. I won't quickly forget Renée Fleming in *Der Rosenkavalier* or Cate Blanchett in *A Streetcar Named Desire*. The excitement generated by ArtPrize in Grand Rapids, Michigan, will continue to inspire me, as will performances by the dance, theater and music ensembles I have had the pleasure of enjoying this year. And how fortunate are we to have diverse arts groups to enjoy from Penumbra Theatre in Minnesota to the Santa Cecilia Orchestra in California, from Pregones Theater in New York to the Ritz Theatre in Florida.

The arts have always provided inspiration during our darkest moments; let us all give thanks that even in this difficult period we have great art to give us solace.

What I Want for Christmas (2010)

This is what I hope Santa Claus brings for Christmas this Saturday:

1. Board members of arts organization who remember their missions. While most arts organizations have missions that relate to bringing arts and arts education to their communities, many board members really believe that the missions of their organizations are to break even. They believe that cutting budgets and doing less is satisfactory as long as the budget is balanced. We need to remember that doing less and doing less important work does not achieve the mission. And, in fact, it works against the possibility of achieving a balanced budget.

2. Arts leaders who focus on training the next generation of arts leaders. We are nearing a dangerous point when an entire generation of arts leaders will retire. This is a very difficult time for the arts because of a challenging economy, an increasing number of electronic substitutes putting pressure on our prices and a generation of young people with no arts background. We need trained, sophisticated arts managers to see the arts world through the next 20 years. The only people who can provide this training are those in the current generation of arts leaders, but we have been so busy running our organizations that we have ignored the needs of our field.

3. Political leaders to remember that almost 6 million Americans are employed in the arts, that we are a main motivator of tourism and that we generate billions of dollars of economic activity. We are not just an effete interest group serving the elite. We are a potent sector of the economy in virtually every community, providing service to all Americans. Arts organizations can help build greater appreciation for our field by doing a better job of institutional marketing. If the work we did in our communities was more visible, it would be harder for political leaders to

dismiss it.

4. Superintendants of schools, school board members and principals who remember that we live in an economy far different from the one when they were in school. The majority of economic activity is no longer tied to manufacturing. We need our children to be creative problem-solvers if they are to be successful and if our nation is to thrive. The arts are a great and inexpensive way to help children exercise their creative muscles. We in the arts need to collaborate with the leaders of our school systems so a meaningful arts education program can be available for every student.

5. Arts organizations that are willing to work together on projects of great impact that surprise and enchant our communities. We are far too competitive with each other. Yet in many communities, we have failed to create broad visibility for our collective work. This hampers our fundraising and ticket-selling activities. We will only thrive if we create work that exceeds the capabilities of any one of our organizations. And then we have a far better chance of achieving our missions.

I know I am being greedy asking for so much.